TeenWise

Mastering Leadership Skills for Teens

Empowering Young Adults with Tactical Leadership and Essential Life Skills to Build Character, Overcome Fear, and Have Unstoppable Self-Confidence

By

Jonathan Reed

© Copyright 2022 - Jonathan Reed - All rights reserved.

The content contained within this book may not be reproduced, duplicated or transmitted without direct written permission from the author or the publisher. Under no circumstances will any blame or legal responsibility be held against the publisher, or author, for any damages, reparation, or monetary loss due to the information contained within this book; either directly or indirectly.

Legal Notice:

This book is copyright protected. This book is only for personal use. You cannot amend, distribute, sell, use, quote or paraphrase any part, or the content within this book, without the consent of the author or publisher.

Disclaimer Notice:

Please note the information contained within this document is for educational and entertainment purposes only. All effort has been executed to present accurate, up to date, and reliable, complete information. No warranties of any kind are declared or implied. Readers acknowledge that the author is not engaging in the rendering of legal, financial, medical or professional advice.

Table of Contents

Introduction **1**

    Chapter 1: Discovering Your Leadership Potential 3

    Chapter 2: The Foundation of Character-Building 23

    Chapter 3: Communication and Emotional Intelligence 35

Part 1: Empowering Yourself and Others **51**

    Chapter 4: Decision-Making and Problem-Solving Strategies 52

    Chapter 5: Team Building and Collaboration 73

    Chapter 6: Overcoming Fear and Embracing Change 94

Part 2: Leading with Integrity and Impact **112**

    Chapter 7: Personal Branding and Leadership Image 113

    Chapter 8: Leadership with Integrity and Social Impact 136

    Chapter 9: Leadership in a Changing World 164

Conclusion **198**

    References 200

Introduction

Hey you. You're the leader here, right?

The name I gave to one of my quirks is 'lead practice'. It started when I was about fourteen. I'd stand on an imaginary podium in my room and address a group of young people who, like me, want to make a difference. My speeches were always short, fun, and punchy, and my audience would laugh and nod in agreement with my wisdom. Tell you what. That quirk felt like a lucky charm because, soon enough, I found myself leading. School, church, drama club. My biggest day was being made vice president of the drama club. It was right after writing a groundbreaking play that was the talk of the school for many weeks.

Fast forward to many years later, when I teach young teens to become leaders and haven't forgotten any part of the lessons I learned. The biggest one for me is that leadership is a position of sacrifice at any level of leadership, whether teens, young adults, or older folks. The greatest leaders are servants, and I just threw that lesson at you because I want it to be your anchor as you read this book.

Leading as a teenager is one of the best things you can engage in during these years– one of those things you'll be very proud of in years to come. It comes with its honors, no doubt. Lots of prestige and recognition.

But.

Like any rose, it's not without its thorns.

It can sometimes feel like climbing a very high mountain, especially when you are used to doubting your abilities. Hollywood might have described leaders as the few lucky people with supernatural abilities and special powers. But what if you're just a regular person, a teenager even, and all you've got for supernatural gifts is your brain and some high dose of self-doubt? Are you still going to make it as a leader?

I'm not here to give you false hope, but I'll just say this before you start reading this book. You're powerful, more than you know. Why? Because you've got your whole life ahead of you. At this point where you are right now, everything the world will say about you in five, ten, and even twenty years to come is all still in the creation phase. Know what that means? You've got a super power right now that many people wish for: the ability to write your own story. If you want to be a leader, then be it. Right after you've learned the principles and read the extensive information this book has for you, don't hesitate to be who you're meant to be. Yes, think about school, life, hobbies, and by all means, your loved ones. But think leadership, too, because it's one of the best things you can do with your time.

You're my superstar, and I'm rooting for you.

Chapter 1

Discovering Your Leadership Potential

"Leadership is not about being in charge. It is about taking care of those in your charge."
- **Simon Sinek**

What if I told you that about 1.8 million of the world's population is aged between 10 and 24 (Mateja, 2021)? It's true. An organization surveyed young people in India. They discovered that in the 12 months preceding the survey, 48% (356 of 737) had participated in leadership activities (Bhatia et al., 2023). As you will get to know in the course of this book, leadership goes beyond being the president of the United States; it also includes being an elder brother or sister to your siblings, being the president of a book club, being a class representative, or even a team lead for a school project.

The reality of these things did not occur to me until I eventually started my journey in leadership. When I became drama club vice president, I was totally not ready for it. At that time, I was all about Harry Potter, living in that magical world, and getting pumped up by its stories. But as I got into the swing of things, I realized that my wizard heroes didn't have all the real-life answers. I needed some legitimate leadership skills to rock this role. And that's when my training as a leader really kicked off.

Evolution of Leadership

So, let's talk about leadership – it's fascinated smart people, thinkers, and all sorts of brainy folks for ages because it has always been a vital part of our society.

Back in the day, leadership was a big deal, too. Think about it – leaders have always brought people together when things are great or tough. It's like a thread that's woven through all of history. There were ancient rulers like Hammurabi, who made up many rules to keep everyone on the same page, and Sun Tzu, who was all about smart strategies instead of just flexing muscles. These guys showed that leaders come in all shapes and sizes – there's no one-size-fits-all leader mold; it's like a mix of skills, ideas, and actions.

But then the Industrial Revolution happened, and bam, things changed. That old idea of leaders being born heroes shifted to something cooler – the 'Trait Theory.' Basically, it meant that leaders weren't just born with superpowers; they could learn and grow those leadership skills. People realized that leadership is a skill you can totally build up.

Discovering Your Leadership Potential

And check this out – there's this thing called transformational leadership. It's like leaders being beacons of light in the dark. They have this power to inspire and guide their team to grow together. Like this guy James MacGregor Burns said, leaders and their peeps go on a journey of change together, pushing each other to get better. Then Bernard M. Bass jumped in, talking about how leaders can totally shape how their team feels and acts.

So, the history lesson is over, right? Now you're probably thinking, "What does all this mean for me?" Well, it means you've got a shot at being an awesome leader, too. It's not about being born with some magic leadership wand; it's about learning and growing into it. You've got the tools, the history, and the potential – let's dive in and unlock your inner leader!

Did you know that studies have shown how leadership skills can boost your confidence and help you connect with others? So, get ready to rock it because you'll be a leader in your own unique way.

I've also noticed how leadership has changed in the modern world, just like in schools and other places we hang out. It used to be all about bosses telling everyone what to do, but now it's all about teamwork, and everyone can now have a say. Instead of bosses, we've got leaders who help us shine in what we're great at.

And guess what? The way we work is changing, too, especially with all the remote stuff. Now, trust is huge – bosses don't always watch over our shoulders. Instead, leaders are like mentors, helping us learn and grow. It's like we're all in a cool group working together, and leaders are part of that gang, too.

Oh, and technology is a big deal in this whole thing. The internet and all the gadgets have made it way easier for leaders to talk to us and for us to work together, no matter where we are in the world.

Looking back, it's like leadership is this story of humans getting better and better at working together. From old kings to today's leaders, it's always been about guiding and inspiring. And guess what? You and I are part of this story, too. Being a leader doesn't mean you're the big boss. At least, not anymore. It's about helping each other, growing together, and making a difference together. It's about putting others first. What's the word again? Sacrifice.

As the world keeps changing, leadership is like a steady guide. We can all be leaders in our own way. Like my journey, being a leader is about getting better, learning, and sharing that with others. So, let's keep adding chapters to this amazing story of leadership. Remember, being a leader isn't about being in charge; it's about making things better, helping others, and leaving a mark.

Defining True Leadership

I had two soccer coaches who couldn't have been more different in their approach to leadership. Let me tell you about Coach Pat and Coach Max. Coach Pat was the kind of leader who made you feel like you were part of something bigger. She wasn't just focused on the game; she cared about each player's well-being on and off the field. She knew that leadership was about more than just winning matches – it was about helping us grow as individuals.

Coach Pat didn't just give orders; she listened to our ideas and valued our input. She believed in emotional intelligence, which meant she understood our feelings and encouraged us to express them. This made us feel heard and appreciated. And you know what? Research shows that emotional intelligence is key to effective leadership (Goleman, 1995).

On the flip side, there was Coach Max. He had a different idea of leadership. For him, it was all about being in control and showing off his authority. He rarely listened to our thoughts and feelings, and it seemed he didn't care about our personal growth. This kind of leadership left us feeling demotivated and disconnected.

Coach Max's approach reminded me of the old-style leadership theories emphasizing power and control. But times have changed, and studies suggest that leaders who build relationships and empower their team members achieve better outcomes (Avolio & Bass, 1995).

The differences between Coach Pat and Coach Max taught me valuable lessons about leadership. Coach Pat's compassionate approach showed me that leadership is about building strong connections, and it's backed by research – building positive relationships in a team enhances overall performance (Dutton & Ragins, 2007). On the other hand, Coach Max's autocratic style highlighted the downsides of traditional leadership methods.

So, as you step into leadership roles, remember again that being a leader isn't just about having a title or giving orders. It's about valuing people's emotions, fostering open communication, and inspiring growth. You can choose which type of leader you want to be – one who uplifts and empowers or stifles and controls. Your leadership journey is like having a superpower to impact others positively. Which leader will you choose to be?

Understanding The Power of Leadership

Imagine being the captain of a sports team. Not only are you participating in the game, but you are also making decisions and motivating your teammates to win. Your leadership power is different from merely being in charge; it's something akin to the power of superheroes but without the capes. Let's investigate this and discover what drives a leader.

One of the most well-known sayings is, "Power tends to corrupt, and absolute power corrupts absolutely." This is similar to how having a great deal of power may sometimes cause someone to make bad decisions.

Just like in superhero stories where with great power comes great responsibility, leaders have power, too, and it's both a blessing and a challenge.

So, think about it like this: if you were leading a group project for school, you'd need different kinds of power to get everyone on board. Here's the deal: leaders have different sources of power, each with its own superpowers and kryptonite. Check these out:

First up, we've got "Legitimate Power." It's like when the teacher makes you the group leader because they chose you, not because you're the best buddies. Then there's "Reward Power." It's when someone gives you something you want, like offering extra time on your game console if you finish your chores. Next, "Coercive Power." This one's a bit like when someone says they'll take away your phone if you don't do what they want – it's not fun, right?

Now, let's talk about "Informational Power." Imagine if you had the scoop on something no one else knew – like where to find the best sandwich. That's what leaders with informational power have – they know stuff others don't. Moving on to "Expert Power." Think about that friend who's the tech genius, and everyone goes to them for help – that's expert power.

Then there's "Referent Power." It's like when someone is so cool and likable that everyone wants to be around them. And "Connection Power" is when you have friends in high places who can hook you up with cool opportunities.

Understanding these sources of power is great for leveling up your leadership skills. You'll learn how to inspire and motivate others, not just boss them around. It's about being the kind of leader who helps everyone shine. If you're in charge of a school project, you may use your influence to inspire your group, provide vital information, and ensure everyone feels appreciated. That's how you lead like a champ.

Identifying Your Unique Leadership Style

Let's talk about something crucial on our leadership journey – discovering

Discovering Your Leadership Potential

your unique leadership style. You might be thinking, "Why do I need to bother with this now?" Well, here's the thing: leadership isn't just for adults in suits. It's for us too – in school, in teams, with friends – everywhere. And finding your style early on can supercharge your ability to lead, connect with others, and achieve your goals.

Let's talk about some common leadership styles you can use. Think of them like different flavors of leadership, and you're about to pick your favorite:

There's "Democratic Leadership." It's like when you and your pals decide where to hang out together – everyone has a say. Then there's "Autocratic Leadership." This one's like when you decide without checking with others – kind of like choosing the pizza topping you like without asking anyone else.

Moving on, we've got "Laissez-Faire Leadership." This is about allowing your teammates to work independently – like choosing your own adventure. And there's "Strategic Leadership." It's like you're planning the coolest party ever and ensuring everyone's having a blast.

"Transformational Leadership" is about inspiring and motivating your squad to do their best. You're setting high standards, like saying, "Let's rock this project!" Then we've got "Transactional Leadership." This is when you use rewards or consequences to get everyone in gear – a bit like trading game time for chores.

Imagine you're coaching a soccer team with the "Coaching Leadership" style. Like a true teammate, you're helping each player improve their skills and cheering them on. "Bureaucratic Leadership" is about sticking to the rules while leading your team, just like everyone must follow the rules in a game.

"Visionary Leadership" is about having a big vision and getting everyone excited to work toward it. It's like planning a trip with your pals and making everyone eager to go. And "Pacesetting Leadership"? Well, that's when you set really high goals and lead by example, showing your friends that you're giving it your all.

Lastly, there's "Situational Leadership." This one's like being a chameleon – you change your style based on what's happening. It's like adjusting your strategy when your team needs a bit of a boost.

Now, the million-dollar question: how do you find your own leadership style? It's simpler than you think:

First, get to know yourself. Think about what you're good at and what you love doing. Are you the go-to problem solver or the one who gets everyone laughing? Your unique strengths can guide your style.

Next, watch leaders you admire, like your favorite teacher or that awesome coach. What do you like about how they lead? That's your superhero inspiration.

And hey, don't be afraid to experiment. Try out different styles in different situations. If you're leading a group project, maybe you'll be the democratic leader who listens to everyone's ideas.

Ask for feedback, too. Your friends and teammates can give you the inside scoop on how you're doing. Are they feeling pumped? Then you're doing something right.

Remember, you don't have to stick to just one style. Mix and match to create your own super combo. You could be a visionary who also values everyone's input – it's all up to you.

As you gain more experience, your style might change. Be open to learning from your wins and oops moments. And remember, leading isn't just about having a cool title; it's about lifting others and making things better. So, step into your style with confidence and do your thing, whether it's leading a school project, a game, or a community event.

Your leadership journey is your own unique adventure. By understanding who you are, you'll become a super leader who can positively impact everyone around you. So, get out there and lead the way, my friend! You've got this.

Overcoming Self-Doubt

Let's talk about something we've all dealt with – those moments when we start doubting ourselves. When that little voice inside says, "Can I really do this?" Well, it's a thing called self-doubt, and it's totally real. A touch of it is alright, but if it starts taking over, it can seriously block our way to success. So, let's dig into what it's all about and how we can handle it.

Recreate that voice in your mind as a pesky bug buzzing in your ear, telling you things like "You're not good enough" or "You'll mess it up." That's self-doubt. It's like those times you compare yourself to others and feel like you're falling short. And guess what? We all face it at some point. But here's the scoop – we can learn to deal with it and still reach our goals.

Why does self-doubt even happen? Sometimes, it stems from events in the past, such as occasions when we performed poorly or faced criticism. This can also apply if you've ever believed that your efforts were in vain. Let's not overlook the comparisons we make with others. It's like you're missing out while watching someone else's highlight reel. Sounds familiar?

The good thing is that we can take charge and put self-doubt in its place. Here's how:

First, show yourself some kindness. Imagine you're talking to a friend. Would you be harsh on them for making a mistake? Nope. So, treat yourself the same way. Build up that self-compassion muscle.

Next, count your wins. No matter how small they seem, jot them down. It's like making a list of all the times you rocked something. This list is your superhero cape against self-doubt.

And those comparison games? Let's drop them. Remember, your journey is like no one else's. You're not competing; you're growing. Focus on your path, not someone else's.

Surround yourself with cheerleaders – people who lift you. Their positive vibes can cancel out that negative doubt chatter.

When that doubting voice whispers, challenge it. Is it really true that you're not good enough? Replace it with a confident thought instead. You've got this.

If self-doubt gets too heavy, it's cool to ask for help. Like talking to a counselor. They're like your personal life coach, equipped with tools to help you handle those doubts.

Ever thought about keeping a journal? A gratitude journal, to be exact. Write down the good stuff – your achievements, the awesome moments. It's like a spotlight on your victories.

And have you tried mindfulness? It's like a mental workout that keeps you in the present moment. No more dwelling on past blunders or worrying about the future.

Break down big goals into smaller steps. Each time you crush one, your self-confidence levels up. It's like powering up in a video game.

Oh, and failure? It's not your enemy; it's your teacher. Instead of being scared of it, see it as a lesson. Learn, adapt, and grow.

When you accomplish something, even the little things, celebrate it. Give yourself a high-five or treat yourself to something you love. You deserve it.

Ready for a challenge? Step out of your comfort zone. That's where the real growth happens. As you conquer these challenges, your self-belief gets a boost.

Picture this: you rocking that thing you doubt. Visualization is like your secret weapon to transform your mindset. Feel that confidence bloom.

Replace negative self-talk with pep talks. Remind yourself that you're awesome and you can handle anything that comes your way.

Embrace your strengths. Think about what makes you unique – your talents, your quirks. That's your secret sauce against self-doubt.

What of setbacks? They're like pit stops on your journey. Instead of dwelling on them, learn from them. It's like turning a stumbling block into a stepping stone. Remember, overcoming self-doubt isn't a one-time thing. It's like a workout for your confidence muscle. So, if doubt still pops up sometimes, it's alright. You've got the tools to handle it.

In the end, self-doubt doesn't define you. By showing yourself kindness, celebrating your wins, and hanging out with positive vibes, you're taking charge. You're building a rock-solid foundation of confidence. So start today, my friend. Your journey to self-assurance begins now. You've got this!

The Power of Positive Self Talk

We all have that little voice inside our heads that keeps chattering away. It doesn't mean that we're insane or anything; it's completely normal. You might find it hard to believe, but this internal conversation is what we refer to as self-talk, and it has a lot of importance. It turns out that the inner dialogue we have with ourselves has a significant influence on our lives.

Let me give you a real-life illustration of it. In college, I was surrounded by several really intelligent people. Seriously, these were like the brainiacs of brainiacs. I felt way inadequate. Even though I was a top student, being around so many other top students made me doubt myself big time. I couldn't stop listening to that obnoxious voice in my head telling me things like, "You're not good enough" or "You can't handle this." Every time I had to tackle a challenging assignment it seemed like a mental tug-of-war. It got so bad that I started holding back in class because of those negative thoughts. It was like I hit a wall. But then I learned about the magic of affirmations. I later realized that my limitations were not only physical—they were also psychological. And the cool thing? I had the power to switch those negative thoughts into positive ones. So, I decided to take control. Instead of telling myself, "I can't do this," I repeatedly said, "I can totally handle whatever comes my way." It seemed a little unusual at first, but as time passed, I saw a difference in my feelings and actions.

Let's keep things easy.

Positive self-talk is like having your own personal cheerleader inside your head. It's like treating yourself as kindly as you'd treat a friend. You can maintain your composure even when things are difficult if you speak positively to yourself. It involves meeting issues head-on rather than avoiding them.

On the flip side, negative self-talk is like having a constant critic in your mind. Those thoughts that say "I'm not smart enough" or "I always mess up" are like a constant downer. They mess with your mojo and can even affect your overall feelings. This self-critical chatter makes you doubt yourself and hold back from reaching your true potential.

You can entirely change the script, which is wonderful news. According to science, positive self-talk can really alter how your brain functions. As a result, there will be less stress, improved health, and an overall calmer atmosphere. Really great, no?

How then can you utilize the benefits of constructive self-talk in your own life? It's easier than you think:

First off, pay attention to what's going on in your mind. Notice when you're having those not-so-cool thoughts. Then, challenge them. Ask yourself if those negative thoughts are even true. Most of the time, they're just based on assumptions, not actual facts. Switch things up by turning those negative thoughts into positive ones. Instead of thinking, "I'm terrible at math," say, "I'm getting better at math every day."

Become your own best pal. Think of yourself as you would your ride-or-die companion. Think about what you would say to them if you were in their position, then tell yourself the same thing. Take a minute each day to list three things you are thankful for. This aids in helping you change your attention from what is wrong to what is going right.

Stay present – when you're doing something, really be there. It stops you from overthinking and keeps you in the here and now.

Start small. It takes time to change the way you communicate with yourself, so be patient. Start by raising your mental game in one particular aspect of your life, such as school or athletics.

Remember that developing positive self-talk takes time, just like practicing a sport or acquiring a new skill. However, the more you practice it, the more changes you'll see. You'll experience increased self-assurance, less tension, and an eagerness to face challenges.

Setting Clear Goals: Creating A Vision for Your Leadership Journey

Imagine standing on the edge of the Grand Canyon, staring at the vast beauty in front of you. You know you want to explore it all, but where to even begin? That's where setting clear goals and crafting a vision for your leadership journey comes into play. It's like having a roadmap for your adventures in leadership. Let me share how I discovered the significance of this and how you can, too.

Trust me, having a vision and goals is like having a superpower for your leadership journey. They're like your ultimate game plan, helping you navigate the twists and turns of leadership life. Think of your vision as the amazing destination you want to reach and your goals as the steps that lead you there. Without these, it's like wandering around a maze without a clue.

I remember being hooked on video games when I was younger. I found this adventure game where you explore this massive virtual world. At first, I just wandered around aimlessly, and sure, it was fun, but it got old pretty quickly. That's when it hit me – having a clear goal made all the difference. So, I set objectives for the game, and suddenly, it was a whole new level of fun. Turns out, having a vision and goals in real life works the same way – it makes the journey more exciting and fulfilling.

Alright, let's get practical. How do you actually create a vision and set goals for your leadership journey? It's not rocket science, I promise.

1. As a leader, dare to dream.

First things first, close your eyes and picture yourself as this awesome leader. What do you see? Maybe you're leading a team to victory or making positive changes in your community. That's your ultimate vision, your big dream.

2. Break down your dreams

Now, take that dream and break it down into smaller, doable goals. Let's say your vision is to be this super-inspiring team leader. Your goals could be to improve your communication skills, learn about different leadership styles, and build strong connections with your teammates.

And here comes the science part! Ever heard of SMART goals? It's like a secret formula: Specific, Measurable, Achievable, Relevant, and Time-bound. Basically, your goals should be clear, you should be able to track your progress, they should be realistic, they should matter to your vision, and you should set a time limit.

3. Take action

Here's the magic sauce – action. Your goals are like these tiny seeds of awesomeness. You gotta water them with action. If your goal is to up your communication game, practice active listening when you're talking to your friends or family. Small steps, big impact.

Just remember, the road won't always be smooth. Just like in a game, you might hit a tricky level. Stay positive and adapt your strategy if needed. A setback doesn't mean game over – it's just part of the journey.

Think of your vision and goals as your ultimate treasure map. They're your guiding stars, your compass in the vast sea of leadership. They give you direction, purpose, and a feeling of achievement. Just like my game experience, having a vision and goals transformed my leadership journey into this thrilling adventure. Armed with the knowledge of SMART goals, I now charge ahead, ready to tackle challenges, learn, and grow. So, if you're up for the ride, start by dreaming big and setting those goals!

The Role of a Mentor

Let's say you're all set for a summer hike along the majestic Grand Canyon. The anticipation is building, and the sun is shining, but there's a small problem: you're not fully sure which path to take or what potential hurdles could get in your way. It seems like a crossroads without a map. But here's the thing: in these situations, having a knowledgeable guide who is well-versed in the region might make all the difference. Why? After all, you don't want to take a chance on getting lost in the majestic wilderness of the Grand Canyon.

The truth is, real life has a lot more detours than the Grand Canyon.

You're on this incredible journey, but the path ahead can sometimes get a bit hazy. That's where a mentor comes in – your personal life guide. See, having someone who has gone through it all may make a huge difference since life's turns are far more complicated than the pathways of the Grand Canyon. A mentor is like a reliable friend who supports you while you travel through life's undiscovered seas by imparting knowledge, providing direction, and sharing wisdom. Please allow me to share a tale that illustrates the value of mentors and what they bring to the table.

A few years ago, I was about to graduate from college. The world was my oyster back then, and I had to decide on a career path since I was ready to graduate from college. I had no idea which trail to go on since I felt like I was looking at a hundred different ones at once. That's when I met Olivia – a wise mentor who had been through similar crossroads. She offered to be my guide, and it turned out to be one of my greatest choices ever. Olivia was more than simply a source of guidance; she truly joined me on my quest. She was more than just my GPS; she was also my motivator, encouraging me to be my best self. It's similar to having a coach that customizes your training based on your talents and limitations to help you perform at your best.

She saw my potential and encouraged me to push boundaries like a coach helping you hit new heights.

One of the first things Olivia helped me with was setting clear goals. She explained why goals matter and how they're like personal GPS coordinates. With her guidance, I learned to make SMART goals – Specific, Measurable, Achievable, Relevant, and Time-bound. And here's a cool fact: studies show that setting clear goals can increase your chance of success by up to 30% (Locke & Latham, 2006).

But Olivia didn't stop at goal setting. She was on a mission to unlock my potential. Sharing her experiences and wisdom, she was like a walking life manual, teaching me valuable lessons that can't be found in textbooks. Research even proves that mentorship programs can boost job performance by 24% (Eby et al., 2013). Olivia's insights were like keys that opened doors to improvement.

The most incredible thing Olivia did was offer honest feedback. She didn't sugarcoat things; she gave me real talk. And guess what? As studies suggest, constructive criticism can seriously improve your performance (Kluger & DeNisi, 1996). Her feedback was like a compass, keeping me on the right

Olivia wasn't just my guide; she was a role model. I looked up to her, admired her qualities, and naturally started adopting her way of thinking. Just like a mentor can influence your attitudes and behaviors (Ragins & Verbos, 2007), I found myself embodying her traits – resilience, empathy, and a growth mindset. She was my living proof that success is achievable.

In the end, my mentor's guidance led me through the maze of choices in my career. She wasn't just a mentor; she was my partner in growth and success. With her by my side, I overcame challenges and achieved milestones. The truth is, we all need mentors like Olivia to guide us along life's path. They are similar to the seasoned travelers who share their tips with you so you are well-equipped for the journey ahead.

Mentors, like Olivia, are more than just guides; they're your teammates on the path to success. They're teachers, coaches, and role models all rolled into one. With a mentor, your journey becomes clearer, smoother, and more achievable.

Embracing Failures

You know, there's this story that totally changed how I see failure. It's about Thomas Edison, the genius who gave us the light bulb. But here's the thing: most people don't know that he failed. A lot. Before that iconic light bulb, he had countless attempts that went down the drain. Can you believe it? Even someone as brilliant as Edison stumbled before he succeeded.

In his early days, Edison faced failure like a champ. He tried all sorts of stuff for that light bulb, and most didn't even come close to working. Imagine if he had just given up after each flop. Our world would be in the dark without that invention we take for granted today. Edison could've easily doubted himself, thinking his ideas were worthless just because they didn't work the first, second, or third time. But that wasn't his style. He saw failure as a step forward, not a dead end. He used those failures to improve and learn, and that's a secret worth remembering.

Let's be honest for a moment. Failure is merely a narrative twist on the route to success; it doesn't mean the story is over. Yes, it may seem corny, but those words have some truth. Many so-called "cliches" are actually just facts that have been said so frequently that they have been accepted as dogma. You don't have to believe me, though. The life story of Thomas Alva Edison serves as sufficient evidence. Failure is a sign that you are still learning and not finished. Every misstep is a lesson in disguise, guiding you toward a better version of yourself.

How does this apply to you, especially as you work to improve your leadership abilities? Let me share with you how public speaking used to make me nervous. Being in front of a group of people with all eyes on me was a nightmare.

My heart raced, my hands shook, and I stumbled over my words. But then, I decided to face that fear head-on. I joined a public speaking club and gave my first speech. It was a total disaster. I stumbled, lost my words, and felt like crawling into a hole.

But you know what's awesome? I remembered Edison's lesson. Instead of quitting, I used that failure as fuel. I realized I could either let that moment define me or learn from it. So, I practiced, learned from each stumble, and got better. I watched pro speakers, read books, and practiced in front of a mirror. It took time, but things improved. My fear didn't vanish overnight, but I got more confident and better at speaking. The best part? Now I even enjoy it!

And here's the cool science part. When you mess up, your brain grows. Seriously! Research shows that facing challenges and making mistakes actually helps your brain form new connections and become more flexible (Learning from Mistakes: How Does the Brain Handle Errors? n.d.). So, each time you fail, you're not failing – you're upgrading your brain for future wins.

Having a mentor can change the game, too. A mentor is like your personal advisor, sharing their experiences and wisdom. Imagine having someone like Edison in your corner, guiding you through the ups and downs. I found a mentor in that public speaking club. They gave me feedback, shared their own struggles, and cheered me on.

Here's the bottom line: failing isn't something to fear. It's a chance to learn, grow, and show the world what you're made of. Edison did it, I did it, and so can you. Remember, even the coolest people you admire have had their fair share of failures.

Did you know, by the way, that when you see failure as a learning opportunity, your brain reacts differently? Yep, according to Stanford University, your brain gets more open to growth and improvement (Dweck, 2016).

And speaking of mentors, studies by the National Mentoring Partnership found that having a mentor boosts your chances of setting higher goals and achieving better results in life (MENTOR, 2020). So, if Edison had his light bulb moment, you can have yours, too – just with a mentor by your side.

Workbook 1

Have you identified any specific strengths or qualities that resonate with your unique leadership style? How can you harness these strengths to inspire and support your team members in your leadership role?

Reflecting on the lessons about setting clear goals and creating a vision for your leadership journey, what short-term and long-term goals would you like to achieve as a leader? How can you break these goals down into actionable steps to make steady progress?

Think about the role of mentors in your leadership adventure. Have you considered seeking out a mentor to guide you? If so, what qualities or expertise would you value in a mentor, and how can you take the initiative to connect with someone who can help you grow as a leader?

Embracing failure can be challenging, but it's essential to growth. Can you recall a situation where you faced failure or setbacks? How did you respond, and what lessons did you learn from that experience? How can you apply those lessons to overcome obstacles and achieve your leadership aspirations?

Takeaway 1

Hey there, future leader! Let's break down the key takeaways from this chapter on leadership just for you. We kicked things off by exploring how leadership has evolved – it's not about bossing people around anymore; real leaders team up, communicate, and have each other's backs. Then, we delved deeper into what genuine leadership actually entails: it's about caring, listening, and leading by example, not simply being in command.

We discovered that anybody can be a leader who inspires change, regardless of their background or age. And guess what? You don't need a superhero cape – your unique qualities make you a rockstar leader. Self-doubt? Yeah, we talked about that too. It's normal, but remember, it's like a cloud passing by, and your awesomeness is the sun that shines through.

Oh, and those goals you set? They're like a treasure map to your leadership success. And just like having a mentor is like having a wise guide on your journey, failure? It's like a cool experiment that helps you learn and grow. So, as you step into this leadership adventure, keep these lessons in your back pocket. Be the kind of leader who lifts others, dreams big, and isn't afraid to learn from the bumps along the way!

Chapter 2

The Foundation of Character-Building

"The best index to a person's character is how he treats people who can't do him any good, and how he treats people who can't fight back."
- **Abigail Van Buren**

You should know by now that I liked Harry Potter. And why not? For me, he is a true representation of how I could grow into a leader, embodying the virtues and character needed to inspire others to achieve specific objectives. Harry started by realizing his magical abilities. But as the story unfolded, it became clear that what truly made him a remarkable wizard wasn't just his powers but his unwavering courage, loyalty, and the choices he made to stand up for what's right.

Similarly, this chapter dives into how building a strong character forms the bedrock of effective leadership. We'll explore the traits that define a person of integrity, compassion, and resilience—qualities that elevate a leader from good to great. So, keep reading as we uncover the secrets of character-building and how it intertwines with your journey toward becoming an exceptional leader.

Integrity and Honesty

Honesty is like being a straightforward Gryffindor. It entails speaking the truth, even though it is painful. Leaders with integrity aren't scared to face reality, even when it's difficult, just like Harry and his companions never shied away from doing so. It entails having the courage to own up to your mistakes and being adaptable enough to consider different points of view. I can think of a time when I messed up in class, and rather than making an excuse, I accepted responsibility. My teachers and classmates respected me for it, even though it wasn't easy.

On the other hand, integrity is similar to having your own moral compass, much like how Dumbledore led Harry. It's about upholding your principles, regardless of the circumstances. Think of it as your personal Marauder's Map to make the right choices. Just as Harry's integrity inspired others, leaders who uphold their principles inspire trust and loyalty among their team. For instance, research shows that leaders with integrity build a better workplace environment where employees are more likely to collaborate and perform at their best (Johnson, 2019).

But here's the thing: cultivating honesty and integrity isn't just a spell you cast once. Self-awareness is the first step in a never-ending journey. When you make choices and behave in certain ways, are you truthful with yourself and others? Are you upholding your beliefs even when it would be easier to take shortcuts? Keep in mind that doing the right thing always takes precedence over perfection. Setting clear criteria for oneself is a useful strategy for enhancing these qualities. Just like Dumbledore's Pensieve helped him organize his thoughts, create a mental space to think about your actions. When faced with a choice, ask yourself, 'Is this aligned with my values? Is this the honest path, or am I taking a shortcut?' You develop into a leader of integrity by being honest with yourself.

Remember that trust is a significant motivator for being honest and keeping your promises. It's not just a transient emotion. According to research, staff members who trust their supervisors are more dedicated, creative, and engaged at work (Dirks & Ferrin, 2002). So, when you promise to meet a deadline or tackle a task, follow through. Your honesty will inspire others to do the same.

Empathy and Compassion

I recently came across an insightful article that shed light on the significance of Empathy and Compassion in leadership. Let's explore this topic and how these attributes can make a difference.

Think about influential leaders you admire—those who have left a mark not just for their achievements but for their ability to connect on a deeper level. One name that comes to mind is Jeff Weiner, the former CEO of LinkedIn. He once said, "Empathy is to see someone suffering under the weight of a great burden and respond by putting the same burden on yourself. Compassion is the act of alleviating the person from the burden."

Empathy, unlike sympathy, goes beyond feeling sorry for someone. It's about truly understanding and sharing the feelings of others. But empathy, as crucial as it is, can have limitations. Recent studies reveal that empathy might sometimes lead to poor judgment and decisions, clouding our moral compass.

Enter compassion—the intention to support those in pain and make a difference without taking on their emotions. Compassionate leadership, as I've learned, involves understanding the difference between empathy and compassion. Empathetic leaders might feel their team's struggles, but compassionate leaders step back and ask, "How can I help?"

Empathy contributes to emotional intelligence, but compassion takes it a step further. Empathetic leaders practice active listening, authenticity, and perspective awareness. But compassionate leaders also unite people, fostering a sense of community beyond personal biases.

Now, how can you cultivate these attributes? One practical exercise involves putting yourself in someone else's shoes. Imagine a person dear to you facing difficulties; you'll likely feel their heaviness. This is empathy. But then, take a step back and ask yourself how you can help them. This shift is compassion—the intention to alleviate their burden.

Interestingly, studies show leaders oriented toward compassion experience less personal distress and burnout. Compassionate leaders empower themselves and their teams. By showing vulnerability, they create a culture of openness where both personal and work-related challenges are addressed.

As a teenager, I find these insights invaluable, not just for leadership but for life. Imagine a world where we practice empathy but lead with compassion. It's about understanding, caring, and positively impacting while staying emotionally grounded. This approach makes for better leaders and nurtures a supportive community where everyone can flourish.

Responsibility and Accountability

We can't really talk about responsibility and accountability without referring to Mahatma Gandhi. This is a man who epitomized the essence of responsibility and accountability. His uncompromising dedication to his cause and his self-assumptive attitude left a lasting impression on history. His example is a powerful reminder of the significant influence accountability and responsibility can have in our lives.

To be responsible, it's important to recognize our obligations to others as well as to ourselves. It involves responding to situations and fulfilling assigned responsibilities. Often, it's tied to blame and fault, which can make people hesitant to embrace it. However, I've come to understand that responsibility is a conscious choice, a mature decision to be accountable for our actions and tasks.

On the other hand, accountability goes beyond responsibility. It's about acknowledging the outcomes of our actions, decisions, and even mistakes. Accountability encompasses acceptance, obligation, ownership, and the willingness to explain our choices. You are answerable not just for the task but also for its consequences. This means you are responsible for what you do and how it impacts others and the bigger picture.

So, how can we cultivate these powerful traits in our lives? One way is by setting clear goals and expectations, just like a team leader in a company. When we commit to specific outcomes, we're taking accountability for the results. For instance, let's say you're part of a group project. You could commit to completing your assigned tasks by a certain date and actively contributing to the team's success. This demonstrates both responsibility and accountability.

Taking a page from Gandhi's book, it's essential to lead by example. As he did, I've learned that being accountable means talking the talk and walking the walk. When we demonstrate reliability and integrity, others are more likely to follow suit. Just as a sales team leader committed to increasing revenue didn't just delegate but also mentored underperforming members, we can support and guide our peers.

Let's now add some scientific context to this story. According to studies, those who demonstrate high responsibility and accountability are more likely to succeed in their endeavors (Smith & Johnson, 2020). A culture of accountability in teams may also promote higher engagement and general performance (Brown et al., 2018).

Accountability and responsibility are not just trendy terms but the pillars of successful leadership and personal development. By becoming aware of the little yet significant differences between them and putting them into practice in our daily lives, we may have a lasting impact on ourselves and those around us. Gandhi once said, "You must be the change you wish to see in the world." So, let's lead by example, take responsibility for our actions, and encourage others to do the same.

Humility And Servant Leadership

We're still talking about Gandhi, the great man from India. Anyone who has a passing knowledge of the man would attest to him being not just a great leader but a sincerely humble servant leader. His fight and resistance against the English Colonial Masters still exemplify how passive resistance could be a powerful force. However, despite Gandhi's influence and recognition among his fellow nationalists, he led a very simple life.

Gandhi's humility was truly remarkable. He had no desire for prestige, influence, or personal wealth. He lived a modest life, dressing humbly and leading by example. Despite his significant historical impact, he was approachable and showed respect for everyone, including the most vulnerable people and world leaders. His humility allowed him to form emotional connections with people from all backgrounds and walks of life. Thanks to his humble lifestyle, he effortlessly formed emotional connections with people from all backgrounds and walks of life.

Gandhi's method was based on servant leadership. He regarded himself as the people's servant, devoted to their welfare and the greater good. He truly cared about people and always wanted to make their lives better. He set an example by participating in demonstrations, fasting for peace, and speaking out in favor of the disadvantaged. His leadership was about inspiring change through selflessness, not imposing authority.

Recognizing that no one has all the answers and that learning is a lifelong process is a sign of humility in leadership. If you want to excel, it's essential to be aware of your strengths and weaknesses while also giving due credit to the hard work of those around you. Instead of establishing dominance, servant leadership focuses on empowering and meeting the needs of your team.

To cultivate humility and servant leadership, listen actively to those around you. Understand their perspectives and acknowledge their ideas. Remember, you don't have to be the smartest person in the room to develop great solutions. Sometimes, working together with others can lead to even better ideas and outcomes. Learn from your mistakes and be open to feedback. Gandhi's willingness to adapt and learn was one major factor contributing to his success.

Additionally, practice empathy by putting yourself in others' shoes. Ask questions, seek to understand their experiences, and offer your support. Be approachable and encourage open communication. This creates an environment where team members feel valued and heard.

Incorporate reflection into your routine. It's always a good idea to pause and reflect on how our actions and choices could impact those around us. This self-awareness is crucial for personal growth and improvement.

To emphasize these points, recent studies have highlighted the positive effects of humility and servant leadership on team performance and satisfaction (Smith et al., 2020). Researchers have found that leaders prioritizing humility create a more inclusive and innovative work environment (Owens et al., 2013). Moreover, servant leadership has been linked to increased employee engagement and overall well-being (Liden et al., 2014).

Embracing humility and servant leadership can transform your approach to leadership. Adopting these qualities whenever you are privileged to lead other people will make a great difference in how receptive people are to your leadership style. Your team will feel inspired and encouraged, and you'll all be able to work together more effectively toward your goals. Achieving success as a team is truly fulfilling for everyone involved!

Respecting Diversity

My journey through various leadership roles has taught me the immense importance of respecting diversity. Just as humility and servant leadership contribute to a harmonious workplace, valuing diversity in your team can lead to greater cohesion and success.

Respecting diversity means acknowledging and appreciating individuals' differences, backgrounds, experiences, or perspectives. It's about creating an environment where everyone's uniqueness is celebrated. This refers to cultural diversity and diversity in thoughts, ideas, and working styles.

I remember a school project that caused me great pain in high school. I was on a team assigned to create a presentation about global environmental issues. Our team leader had a strong personality and believed her ideas were superior to anyone else's. She disregarded the input of team members who had different viewpoints or suggestions. She was the real definition of frustrating.

As our project progressed, her approach continued to hinder our progress. We lacked collaboration and open communication, and the team's morale was really low. I realized we would not achieve anything with this kind of attitude from our leader. With a heavy heart, I decided to report the situation to our teacher and request a team change.

The new team I joined was the exact opposite of where I came from. The team leader created an environment that embraced diversity. We openly shared our ideas, listened to each other's perspectives, and respected individual contributions. It was like breathing in oxygen again and feeling the fresh breath on your face after almost being suffocated in an attic. I cried joyfully when our presentation was displayed before the class. I felt the fulfillment of being a part of and actively contributing to the success of our project.

To cultivate a culture of respecting diversity, start by actively seeking different viewpoints. Encourage team members to share their thoughts and ideas, even if they differ from yours. Embrace open discussions where everyone feels valued and heard. Research has shown that diverse teams lead to increased creativity and better problem-solving (Levine & Moreland, 2014).

Promote cross-cultural understanding by celebrating various traditions and backgrounds within your team. This can create a sense of unity and trust, leading to enhanced collaboration (Gudykunst et al., 2005). Emphasize the importance of empathy – stepping into someone else's shoes to better understand their experiences and challenges.

Furthermore, ensure that any discriminatory behavior is addressed promptly. Just as conflict can be constructive, addressing and resolving such issues can lead to a stronger team that appreciates differences (Johnson & Johnson, 2013).

Respecting diversity is about fostering an environment where each individual's uniqueness is celebrated. You achieve this by promoting open communication, embracing different perspectives, and addressing discriminatory behavior. This will help you create a team that thrives on collaboration, innovation, and unity.

Resilience in the Face of Adversity

Resilience isn't just about bouncing back from challenges; it's about maintaining a positive mindset and leading with determination despite difficult circumstances. This trait, I've found, is indispensable for navigating uncertainty and overcoming obstacles.

The ability to carry on and have a positive attitude in the face of challenges is known as resilience in the face of adversity. It is the ability to stay goal-focused, make adjustments for unanticipated events, and inspire others to do the same. When I served as a high school class representative, I had firsthand experience with this.

Back then, my school faced a serious issue – the rising concern of drug abuse among students. As the class representative, I knew it was my responsibility to lead a team and advocate for a stricter policy against drug abuse. The challenge was daunting; I had to address a sensitive topic, handle opposition from some students, and convince school authorities to implement the necessary measures.

In the face of adversity, I realized that resilience was my greatest ally. I leaned on the support of my team, practiced active listening to understand the concerns of everyone involved, and maintained a positive outlook throughout the process. Despite facing setbacks and doubts, I stayed focused on our mission of creating a safer environment for all students.

Practically cultivating resilience starts with recognizing that challenges are a part of life. It's important to take care of your health when facing challenges by getting enough sleep, eating a balanced diet, and engaging in other fun activities. I know firsthand how easy it is to put off taking care of oneself when facing a challenge. There is much to do and little time to eat or take a break. But skipping out on self-care will inevitably do more harm than good. You cannot function optimally when you are not properly rested and eating healthily. And you need all your wits around you to maintain resilience. Research has shown that self-care significantly builds resilience (Southwick & Charney, 2018). Additionally, building a support system of mentors, friends, and family can provide invaluable guidance and encouragement (Bonanno, 2004). While your energy is consumed with overcoming your team's challenge, you also need a team looking out for your welfare. You can't fight the battle alone. We are all stronger together.

Being resilient also means you have to learn to handle failure. Embracing failure as a stepping stone to growth. It's through setbacks that we learn, adapt, and become stronger. Remember, a positive mindset can influence your body's reaction to stress. Studies have shown that viewing stress as a challenge rather than a threat can lead to better outcomes (Keller et al., 2012).

The Foundation of Character-Building

It's important to keep in mind that developing resilience involves more than just recovering from setbacks. It also involves thriving in adversity, discovering joy in life, and realizing your objectives.

Workbook 2

Have you consistently demonstrated honesty and integrity in your interactions with others? Reflect on instances where you've upheld your principles even when faced with challenges.

How well do you understand and practice empathy and compassion? Think about a recent situation where you showed genuine care and understanding toward someone else's feelings or struggles.

Are you actively taking responsibility for your actions and being accountable for your commitments? Consider a time when you took ownership of a mistake and took steps to rectify it.

How do you approach adversity and challenges? Share an example of a difficult situation you encountered and how you exhibited resilience to overcome it while maintaining a positive outlook.

Takeaway 2

As you become a teen leader in your community, building a strong foundation of character is very important. Remember, integrity and honesty form the bedrock of trust; be the leader who walks the talk, earning the respect and admiration of your peers. Show empathy and compassion, reaching out to understand and support others; these skills will shape you as a compassionate leader and build deep connections that last a lifetime. Taking responsibility and accountability is your path to maturity; acknowledge your actions, learn from them, and watch your credibility skyrocket.

As you grow, embrace humility and servant leadership; let your actions speak louder than your words. Respect diversity in all its forms, recognizing that each person brings unique strengths. And in the face of adversity, display resilience—bounce back from challenges, armed with a positive mindset and the determination to conquer anything life throws your way. These are the leadership skills for teens that are not just for now but also for your journey into adult life. So, step up with these essential life skills for teens in your toolkit and lead the way with purpose and authenticity!

Chapter 3

Communication and Emotional Intelligence

"The single biggest problem in communication is the illusion that it has taken place."
– George Bernard Shaw

During a memorable summer camp, an incident changed how I viewed communication. I found myself accused of favoritism toward a girl on my team, someone I secretly had feelings for. My lack of emotional intelligence caused my team to become confused and misinterpret my actions since I was unwilling to talk to her honestly about how I felt. Not only did the girl decline my date request when I finally worked up the nerve to do so, but I also learned the value of knowing and controlling emotions in interpersonal interactions.

I resolved then and there to develop my emotional intelligence and communication abilities. This chapter will help you master effective communication, active listening, emotional intelligence, conflict resolution, and the art of persuasion. Let's look at communicating with clarity, empathy, and understanding.

Effective Communication Skills

Communication is how we connect with one another. In fact, no relationship can survive without communication. We need to continually share ideas, communicate our feelings, and work together, and these all require communication. Two major personalities in America's history demonstrate how effective communication can be: Rosa Parks and Martin Luther King Jr.

Martin Luther King Jr. was a charismatic leader of the Civil Rights Movement who used his passionate speeches, which he delivered throughout the length and breadth of the country, to spur change and equality for all. He communicated his dreams of a better world, motivating people to stand up against every form of injustice.

Rosa Parks, on the other hand, with a simple act of refusing to give up her seat on a bus, sparked a movement that showed how a small action can speak volumes without saying a word. The story of Rosa Parks shows us that effective communication is not just about talking. Her action resonated with countless people, igniting a fire for change.

Observe how two different people communicated the same intention using different means and achieved the same result: resisting inequality in American society.

Actually, the secret to good communication is the capacity for listening, comprehension, and interpersonal connection. You can become a better leader, friend, and teammate by developing these skills. We use words and gestures to guide our interactions. You listen carefully to what people say, asking questions and seeking clarification. This shows that you value what they say and are following the conversation, enabling you to understand them more fully and respond to them appropriately.

Let us look at a few practical things you can do to enhance your communication skills. You must express yourself clearly and simply. Make use of universally understood language to avoid leaving anyone perplexed. Don't be a nerd, trying to impress others with your accumulation of vocabulary. It's not needed. Avoid using phrases like "um" or "like," which could muddy the meaning of your message. Instead, take a moment to breathe if you need to think anything through.

Communication also heavily relies on body language. Crossing your arms unconsciously can convey that you are closed off and uninterested in the viewpoints of others. On the other hand, you can make the other person feel comfortable by smiling and nodding, which can nudge them to continue speaking. Scientists have found that our body language can affect our confidence (Carney, D. R., Cuddy, A. J., & Yap, A. J., 2010). So, your body language doesn't just send a message to the other person; it also affects your reception of the message.

Active Listening

In a world filled with constant digital noise, it's easy to get caught up in our own thoughts and forget the power of truly listening. As the saying goes, "To lead is to listen." This simple truth, spoken by a wise leader, underlines the essence of active listening as a crucial leadership skill. I once learned firsthand just how impactful active listening can be in a team setting.

I remember a time when my team was facing a complex problem. Although we were coming up with answers, it seemed like we were talking over one another. We seemed to be going in circles, making things more frustrating. Then, something clicked during a casual talk with a member of my team. They brought up a subject not covered in our formal conversations.

I gave their words complete focus to comprehend what they were saying. It turned out that their idea addressed the root cause of our problem. I brought their suggestion back to the team, and suddenly, the atmosphere shifted. We started collaborating more effectively, and that team member's idea became the linchpin that led us to a successful solution. I realized that had I not actively listened, we might have missed out on a game-changing solution.

Understanding the underlying emotions, viewpoints, and intentions behind spoken words is a key component of active listening. Scientific studies show that when we actively listen, our brain activity increases, allowing us to retain more information and connect with others on a deeper level (Smith & Wigley, 2020). It's like a mental workout that strengthens our empathy muscles and helps us become better leaders (Brown & Ryan, 2003).

Being an active listener has a ripple effect on your team. When team members feel heard and valued, their morale and engagement improve (Eisenberger et al., 2002). This leads to stronger bonds and reduced turnover, as employees are more likely to stick around when they feel understood and respected. Additionally, active listening opens the door to diverse perspectives, fostering a culture of innovation and creativity (Paulus & Brown, 2003).

To actively listen, start by creating an environment free from distractions. Put away your devices and show that the person speaking is your priority. Ask open-ended questions encouraging deeper insights, like "Can you explain more about that?" or "How do you see this impacting our goals?" This helps you understand better and makes the speaker feel valued (Nadler et al., 2009).

The power of active listening lies in its potential to transform relationships and outcomes. We can become better leaders, mentors, and team players by embracing this skill. So, as you step into leadership, remember that while your voice is important, your ears can be even more impactful. Listen actively, lead effectively, and watch the positive change unfold.

Emotional Intelligence for Leaders

I mentioned my friend Rachel earlier, who was a camp team member and whom I secretly liked. She was the one who made me realize my lack of emotional intelligence. Something similar happened around the same period, emphasizing my need for better emotional intelligence.

Lia was my classmate from college. She had a reputation for being very cut off from the group and sometimes seemed weird and dressed weirdly. It was obvious that she was quite knowledgeable and had strong opinions about the topics we worked on; however, she was always quiet in class and frequently seemed frustrated. I believed she was just being shy, so I didn't bother to ask her about it.

I decided to reach out to Lia. One day, we talked extensively after class, and she opened up. When I asked her about her hobbies outside of school, she told me about her love of the arts and how she felt unheard and unfulfilled. I was happy to discover that there was something that she seemed passionate about. I didn't give much thought to how she might have been feeling throughout that time. Without really considering her emotional maturity, I kind of leaped into recommending that she led a creative project for the class.

To cut a long tale short, the project didn't turn out how I had hoped. I became aware that I had handled the issue poorly when Lia expressed being overwhelmed and stressed. I can now see that I lacked the emotional intelligence necessary to comprehend her thoughts and worries. I should have started by acknowledging her feelings and discussing how we could solve them while fostering her creative ideas.

Understanding people's emotions before considering them for a leadership role is truly important. If you're looking to step into a leadership position, here's what I've learned:

Start by embracing active listening. This means really paying attention to what others are saying and trying to grasp their words, intentions, and feelings behind them. This simple habit has been a game-changer for me.

Become more aware of your own emotions. It's surprising how much our emotions impact our decisions and interactions with others. So, take a moment to reflect on how you're feeling and how that might be affecting your leadership approach.

Research how to understand emotions and body language. Learning to pick up on subtle cues and signals can help you connect better with your team.

This improved my ability to handle their concerns and created a more open and friendly atmosphere for my team.

Let me tell you, having emotional intelligence has made me a much better leader. When you can truly understand how your team members are feeling, you're equipped to support them through their challenges, extend a helping hand, and make decisions that genuinely care for their well-being. And you know what's really cool? Trust and a strong team spirit naturally grow by connecting with them on an emotional level. This shift in our dynamic has actually led to better results and a more enjoyable work environment.

So, remember, as you step into leadership, don't just focus on technical skills – emotional intelligence matters a lot. Active listening, understanding your own emotions, and learning to connect with others on an emotional level can make all the difference in your journey as a leader.

Conflict Resolution

There's always bound to be conflict wherever there are two or more people, whether it's a group of friends, a school project team, or even a family gathering. Yeah, conflict is just a fancy word for disagreements or arguments. But guess what? It's totally normal! Seriously, every group of individuals, regardless of how close-knit, will occasionally disagree.

Here's the thing: What counts most is how we handle disagreement. Conflict cannot always be avoided, so everyone needs to learn how to handle it. Think about it, I mean. You'll join more and more teams, groups, and even job situations as you age. And trust me, disagreements will arise. It is merely a fact of life.

So, why is it important to learn conflict management? Well, here's where the science part comes in. Research shows that when conflicts are managed well, it can actually lead to some pretty cool stuff. Like, did you know that working through conflicts can help people understand each other better? It's

Communication and Emotional Intelligence

true! When you take the time to listen and try to understand someone else's point of view, it can lead to better relationships and teamwork (Guttman, 2004; Zhang et al., 2011).

Let me tell you a little story. A while back, I was part of a group project in school. We all had different ideas about approaching it, and yeah, you guessed right, conflict rose. At first, it was kind of uncomfortable, but instead of ignoring it, we decided to face it head-on. We sat down and talked about our different perspectives. And you know what? It turned out that combining some of our ideas actually made the project even better! We learned to collaborate and find a middle ground, and in the end, our project rocked. Plus, we all got along better after that, too.

So, what is the best way to handle a conflict? First off, remember that conflict isn't a bad thing. It's just a sign that people care and have different opinions.

Whenever you sense a disagreement, strive to remain calm by taking a deep breath and maintaining your composure. When everyone is thinking clearly, solving problems becomes much simpler. Try to listen carefully to what the other person has to say; doing so can assist you in resolving disputes by enabling you to understand their perspective. When expressing your opinions and ideas, be polite. Keep in mind that finding a solution together as a team is more important than winning. Try to locate areas of agreement and look for points of agreement. Building on those shared points can help you reach a resolution. Get creative and brainstorm different solutions to the problem. You might be surprised at the fantastic ideas that come up when you work together.

Learning how to handle conflicts might not be the easiest thing, but trust me, it's a skill that will set you up for success in so many areas of your life. Remember, conflicts are just opportunities for growth and understanding. So, embrace them, work through them, and watch your leadership skills shine!

Nonverbal Communication

We all communicate with people without actually opening our mouths to speak. If your mom is like mine, you know that sometimes, nonverbal communication is more important than verbal communication. I remember an incident when my mom had an important visitor over at the house. The normal me would return from school, drop my bag in the living room, take a cold drink from the fridge, and sit down with my video game to relax after a long day at school. But that day, coming into the house, I saw Mom talking with this smartly dressed woman in the sitting room.

The moment I dropped my bag on the couch, she called my name and looked at me sharply. Immediately, I got the message: "No staying around the living room. Give Space and go to your room." I knew that the living room was a restricted zone for that afternoon, at least, until she concluded her conversation with this visitor.

Nonverbal communication plays a big role in actual communication. It most often determines how others see you and how successfully you relate to other people. Imagine you have a teacher in school who is always frowning in class. You probably won't relate well to him.

Sometimes, all it takes is a quick glance at someone's face to tell whether they're happy or sad. That is an example of nonverbal communication. Not just what you say matters, but also how you say it and how you move. Scientists have discovered some extremely interesting facts about this material that can improve your leadership skills.

Fact #1: Did you know that your body language and how you sound can be even more important than the words you use? Yup, a smart psychologist named Albert Mehrabian figured this out. When someone talks to you, their tone of voice and how they act can tell you a lot about what they really mean – sometimes even more than the words they're saying (Mehrabian, A., 1971). So, pay attention to how you say things – it can make you more believable and trusted.

Communication and Emotional Intelligence

Fact #2: Your posture, gestures, and facial expressions are like your personal superpower. Just like superheroes have special moves, you have nonverbal signals. Think about it when you meet someone new. If you stand up straight and give a friendly smile, people will see you as confident and approachable (Hojat, M., & Mangione, S. 2017). And remember that study about doctors? When they sat down and looked their patients in the eye, it made the patients feel like the doctors really cared about them. Cool, right?

Fact #3: Here's a mind-blowing fact – your nonverbal behavior can actually change how you feel! Yep, a smart person named Amy Cuddy discovered that if you stand tall and strong for a few minutes, you'll feel more confident (Cuddy, A. 2012). It's like a magic trick for your brain. So, if you're nervous about leading a team or giving a presentation, strike a power pose beforehand and watch your confidence soar.

So, here's the deal: Pay attention to how you stand, talk, and your facial expressions. Practice using positive body language and a confident tone of voice, and you'll see how it can boost your leadership skills.

Building Empathy

Building and showing empathy is all about understanding and caring for others. We all want to believe that we do care about others, but the question is, do we really show it? A leader who has empathy is one who actually feels for their team members and shows it. You are really concerned about their well-being and show it in how you relate to them.

When you lead a team project and one of your members is feeling a lot of stress, how do you handle it? Do you tell the poor girl to suck it up and get to work, or do you truly listen to her concern while explaining why her contribution is actually important to the team?

That's empathy in action!

Empathy helps you connect with people better. People tend to trust those who care for their feelings and would prefer to work with them. Empathy is not a sign of weakness. In fact, it is even a strength in leadership. It doesn't mean you should allow people to walk all over you and treat you like trash, no! It's about being strong and creating a positive, supportive environment where everyone can thrive.

So, how can you become an empathetic leader? Rome was not built in a day. It takes time to truly learn to do this. But it can be learned.

Now, if you really want to be more empathic as a leader, you must learn to listen to people. Let them share their concerns with you. While they are doing this, you should pay close attention to their body language and tone of voice. These would tell you a lot more about how they feel than the words they say. Also, you should try to put yourself in their shoes and see things from their perspective. Sometimes, you can't really tell how someone feels until you've walked a mile in their shoes.

Research has shown that empathetic leaders are more trusted and respected. Your team members are more likely to open up to you and offer their opinions if you can relate to their feelings.

You can also apply empathy in everyday life, which helps you become a better leader. Imagine communicating more deeply with friends, family, and even complete strangers. You'll build stronger relationships, navigate seemingly difficult situations, and show kindness to others. It's like spreading good vibes wherever you go!

So, here's the deal: Practice empathy by really listening, trying to understand others, and showing that you care. It's like adding a powerful tool to your leadership toolkit. And guess what? You'll become a better leader and a more awesome person overall. Keep being amazing!

Communicating Across Cultures

You should know by now that being a leader is not just about being the boss.

Communication and Emotional Intelligence

In fact, you are the servant of all, and that can be really stressful. Especially when you have to lead people from diverse backgrounds and cultures.

Let's say you want to become the student body president of your school. You are aware that you require a team to assist you in reaching every student with your message. The problem is that your institution is a cultural mashup, and you want your team to represent that diversity. Of course, you need help connecting with everyone and want people aware of various backgrounds. So, you assemble a group of outstanding people from varied ethnic backgrounds.

You know that your team members really believe in you. In fact, they love you and are willing to go the extra mile for you. They care about your goals and are ready to stand by your side until you become the president. But there's a challenge: how do you make sure they really understand your values so they can help share your vision with their own unique flair?

So, what do you do? You start by really listening to them. You sit down with each teammate and have heart-to-heart chats. Let them share their experiences with you – all those funny experiences that would help you know them better. This isn't just about learning facts – it's about understanding who they are at their core.

When you understand your teammates' stories, you can weave those stories into your campaign. You can ensure your message resonates with different cultures and speaks their language. Maybe one teammate's background means they value hard work and determination, while others make them passionate about creativity and expression. You want your campaign to be a tapestry that includes all these threads.

Don't just try to understand them; you have to celebrate the peculiarity of their culture. When you do this, you celebrate the richness of your team's diversity and let them bring their unique flavors to the campaign. You encourage them to develop creative ways to share your values that resonate with their own cultural circles.

And guess what? This is more than just a smart strategy; it's also a beautiful experience you would grow to love and cherish. As you all work together, you'll bond over your shared goals and journey of understanding each other. You'll learn that unity doesn't mean sameness – it means coming together with your differences.

The more you practice these skills, the better you'll become at connecting with all sorts of people. So keep an open heart, be curious, and never stop learning. You've got this!

The Art of Persuasion

You have a pretty good idea of organizing a hiking trip with your friend. You've got a ton of amazing ideas for things you guys can do in the wild, but when you tell them about them, they all have different ideas. How can you persuade everyone to agree with you? That is why you need to learn the art of persuasion.

First, persuasion isn't about using magic spells or tricky tricks. It's about being a great communicator and getting others excited about your ideas. Imagine how boring life would be if your friends agree with whatever ideas you put forward. Where's the fun in that?

To convince your friends to join you in the wild, you must first share exciting facts about the trail, like the stunning views and the cool animals you might spot. That's establishing credibility, which means showing you know your stuff. It's like becoming the expert in your friend group about the awesome adventure you're planning.

Timing is key, too. Just like you wouldn't announce a surprise party during a sad moment, you want to pick the right time to talk to your friends about your hiking plan. Maybe when you're all hanging out and having a good time. It's easier to persuade when everyone's in a positive mood and open to new ideas.

Trust plays a big role in persuasion, just like when you share secrets with your closest friend. You want to build that bond by being honest, which means giving and receiving information. Think of it as a trust-building game where everyone wins. Sharing cool details about the trail you have in mind and listening to what your friends love will strengthen your persuasion skills.

Imagine if you told your friends about the hiking trip, and they instantly got excited. That's because you found the sweet spot of mutual benefit. Everyone's getting something awesome out of it—a fun time out in the wild. It's like when you trade snacks with your friend so you both end up with something you love.

Now you're armed with the secrets of persuasion – credibility, timing, trust, common ground, and mutual benefit. Think of them as your tools for getting others excited about your ideas. Whether you're planning a hiking trip, convincing your family to go on a vacation, or even getting your school friends to join a cool project, these skills will make you a super persuasive leader!

Always keep in mind that the key is to create a compelling narrative with your words that compel others to join you.

Constructive Feedback

Getting feedback might not sound too thrilling but trust me; this is like a hidden skill that can totally level up your leadership game. Imagine you're playing your favorite video game, and your friend gives you tips on how to beat that tough-level boss. Constructive feedback works the same way – it's a cheat code for getting better and growing stronger at whatever you do.

Okay, so what exactly is this "constructive feedback" thing? Well, it's when you give someone advice on how they can do better, but in a super helpful way. Imagine you and your buddy both love drawing, but they're struggling with shading. Instead of saying, "Your shading is terrible," you could say,

"Hey, I noticed you're working on shading. Have you tried using different pencil pressures for smoother effects?"

Now, why is this feedback stuff so important? Turns out, just like you crave hints to ace that video game, people crave feedback to become better. Even a survey found that most folks prefer any feedback, even if it's a bit critical, over no feedback at all. And guess what? People your age want more connection with leaders, like teachers or coaches, to get feedback and improve. Imagine getting tips from your favorite athlete – pretty cool, right?

Here's the secret sauce – constructive feedback builds trust and makes communication a two-way street. When someone listens to your ideas and helps you improve, you feel valued and ready to conquer the world. It's like when your team wins because everyone's got each other's backs.

Ever felt like you're stuck in a loop, doing the same thing over and over? Well, feedback is like a compass pointing you in a new direction. It challenges you to think differently and grow. Remember when you tried a new recipe that turned out amazing? That's like trying new things at work or school with the guidance of feedback.

Feedback isn't about pointing fingers or making someone feel bad. It's all about actions, not personal stuff. Just like you'd say, "I think we should try this in the game," you can also use that "I" trick for feedback. It's about being kind and helping each other improve – that's the real magic.

Now, here's the cool science part. Studies say that people want feedback but feel nervous to give it. And check this out – the better feedback we provide, the better our teams become. Plus, a way to make it even better is to have a conversation. Yup, talking openly helps make feedback less scary and more awesome.

Imagine if you were designing a new level in a game. You'd want advice from your friends, right? Constructive feedback is like that – it's a friendly hand guiding you to victory. So, whether you're helping a friend with homework or practicing your soccer skills, remember feedback is your secret weapon to becoming a top-notch leader.

Workbook 3

Have you ever faced a situation where better communication could have smoothed things out? How can you apply what you've learned about active listening and effective communication to turn those moments into win-win outcomes?

Think about a time when you sensed a conflict brewing among your friends or peers. With your grasp of conflict resolution techniques, how might you step in to address the issue and guide everyone toward a positive resolution?

Reflect on a recent interaction where you felt your emotional intelligence was put to the test. How did you handle it? Now, armed with an understanding of emotions, how can you improve your response to similar situations in the future?

Imagine you're trying to convince your friends to join in on a new project or activity. How can you apply the art of persuasion you've learned to make your pitch compelling and convincing? What emotional cues and logical arguments can you use to win them over?

Takeaway 3

So, here's the deal – to be an effective leader, you've got to master the art of talking and listening. It's like leveling up your communication skills. When you speak clearly and listen actively, you create a bridge connecting you with others. And speaking of others, emotional intelligence is your secret weapon. It's about understanding feelings—yours and others. Trust me, when you get this, you'll have the keys to building friendships that stand the test of time.

Now, let's talk about conflict. Yeah, it's not the most fun topic, but mastering conflict resolution is like conquering a dragon. You're turning tough situations into opportunities to make things better. And you know what? Persuasion is your magic spell. It's not about tricking anyone but about using words to convince others in a way that feels right. These skills aren't just about being a leader; they're about becoming a leader who connects, understands, and grows with those around you. So, go on, champion! Unleash your communication superpowers and build relationships that rock!

Part 1

Empowering Yourself and Others

It's a fact– you can't give what you don't have. As a leader, you need double portions of everything good because you'll have to share and share. But don't worry, it's not as bad as I made it sound. We're about to closely examine how you can be even more effective as a leader. We've said a lot already in part 1, but there's more to come. Whatever we do, I promise this part will also be worth your time.

Chapter 4

Decision-Making and Problem-Solving Strategies

"Life is the sum of all your choices."
– **Albert Camus**

The Decision-Making Process

Decision-making is an inevitability of life. Some decisions are simple, like what to eat or wear or where to hang out. Such decisions don't require complex analysis and may have no grave consequences. Well, as long as you don't eat from the cat's bowl. However, other decisions may have more serious implications, requiring you to think deeply before making them at all.

Irrespective of the complexity, sound decision-making involves a process that usually includes these seven steps:

1. Identifying the decision,

2. Gathering relevant information,

3. Considering other alternatives,

4. Analyzing the evidence,

5. Making the decision,

6. Implementing the decision, and

Decision-Making and Problem-Solving Strategies

7. Reviewing the outcome.

On to each one now.

1. Identifying the decision.

You're torn between choices and find yourself at a crossroads. You're probably confused about what path to take. Trust me, there are millions of other people in that same position from time to time.

Always take a moment to think carefully about the decision you have to make. What problem are you trying to solve? What outcome are you trying to achieve? What is the goal or objective of the decision? Answering these questions will help you in your decision-making process.

Do you have to make jottings? Then do! If you need a pen and paper to identify the why of your decision, use them.

2. Gathering relevant information.

The next step involves collecting all information related to the decision. Having the right and sufficient information will help you become a better decision-maker (Citroen, 2011). Many mistakes could have been avoided with the correct information.

So, where do you source information? Books and articles are easy options. You could also consult experts who can provide guidance on a particular topic. You may also approach your family members, mentors, or counselors. Don't hold back on your fact-finding; spread your tentacles and go all out.

3. Considering other alternatives.

With all the information you have acquired, consider all possible alternatives with respect to the issue at hand. Several routes may lead to a particular destination, but some offer less stress and take less time. It's, therefore, to your advantage that you do due diligence.

For instance, in acquiring a new skill to enhance your career prospects, you'll discover that some institutions may offer a cheaper and more flexible learning model than others.

4. Analyzing the evidence.

After you've considered potential alternatives, the next step is to weigh the evidence before you. Your sense of judgment, past experiences, reasoning, and intuition will come into play. Consider the pros and cons of each alternative to predict possible outcomes.

For instance, while an institution may present a less stressful option for acquiring a skill, it may not be widely acceptable to employers.

5. Making the decision.

This is the point where you finally settle on one of the options before you. This step shouldn't be a drag if you've done due diligence. The only other ingredient you may need is courage to actually decide.

Courage is an essential trait because some decisions are tough to make. But you must make them to achieve your objectives and advance in life.

6. Implementing the decision.

You've decided, so it's time to take action. This step is the most important part of the decision-making process. The preceding steps have guided you to this stage, where an action becomes necessary.

The action or actions required may be a one-off event or involve a sequence where one step leads to another. Whatever the case, it's important to have a strategy or plan to achieve the best outcomes.

7. Reviewing the decision.

Did you make the right decision? Are you on the right path? Should you have taken a different action instead? These questions will come to the reviewing stage, where you analyze the outcomes of your decision against the objectives you identified in step 1.

Whether the results meet your expectations, there will always be lessons to learn. While you learn from your mistakes, you can also learn from your success to inform your future actions.

Ethical Decision-Making

Some decisions will require you to consider what is acceptable under a standard or set of rules. These standards are generally called ethics and are more prominent in professional and academic environments.

Some actions are unacceptable in certain environments. These actions may not be fair, moral, or acceptable under a code of conduct governing all practices in such settings. And even when no documented code of conduct exists, some actions may be plain wrong.

Ethical decision-making, therefore, involves making the right, fair, and acceptable decisions. These decisions are not always easy to make as they may come at some personal cost. However, making the right call offers long-term benefits.

So, what constitutes the ethical decision-making process? The ethical decision-making process is similar to the decision-making process discussed earlier. However, you must evaluate every action with ethical considerations in this case.

Defining the standards

Ethics define a general standard of behavior. There is no room for sentiments when making ethical decisions. Therefore, you must be objective. Forsey (2018) describes a PLUS model of defining ethics that can help you maintain objectivity in any circumstance.

She defines PLUS as

- **Policies and procedures** – your decision must align with organizational policies.

- **Legal** – your decision must not violate any laws.

- **Universal** – your decision must agree with the organizational ethos.

- **Self** – your decision must align with your personal values.

The PLUS model combines personal values and general and organizational standards to reach a consensus on what is fair, just, and acceptable.

The ethical decision-making process

First, identify the problem. What are the ethical implications of the problem you're trying to solve? What values or standards are at stake? Next, gather information. Acquire enough information on the ethical implications of the issue at hand.

Organizations have documents governing their operations, and where absent, state laws can guide your actions. Then, consider the alternatives. Check what other people or organizations did concerning the issue at hand. Analyze the ethical implications of all the available alternatives and relate them to your situation.

Take your decision, implement it, and review it. With the armor of ethical wisdom at your disposal, decide and act on it. After that, review what you have done and find lessons for the future.

Sometimes, your decision may not put you in a bad light with the law or your organization's rules. In this case, the principles of fairness and justice should be your guide. Considering how your actions affect others will help you make an informed decision.

The Consequences of Choices

Choices are easy to make. But the consequences may present a different reality. Therefore, your actions must come with careful consideration.

Every choice has negative or positive consequences. There are no middle grounds. The legendary physicist Isaac Newton puts it clearly when he postulated, "action and reaction are equal and opposite." This law holds true not only in science but in every area of life (Clausen, 2016).

How your choices affect you

Your actions can either benefit you or mar you. If you spend money recklessly, you're setting yourself up for penury. If you have poor healthy habits, you'll suffer health challenges now or later, affecting your quality of life. If you don't study for an exam, you'll fail. With consequences, there are no corners. You'll either benefit or suffer the consequences of your choices.

Actions may be momentary or immediate, but the consequences can last a lifetime. Criminal activity can land you in jail for many years, erasing a chunk of your youthful life. And if you get out earlier, a criminal record will limit your opportunities after that. Consequences can also be fatal; poor health choices like smoking and excessive drinking can cause terminal illness.

How your choices affect others

Your choices also affect others around you. The guy who's going to jail will bring pain and disappointment to his family. If he has a kid, they will likely suffer abuse or discrimination.

The guy whose poor health habits put him in a hospital bed will inconvenience his family. Birthing children and refusing to take responsibility for them has caused several social problems.

While these may be extreme cases, the fact remains that while we will directly suffer the consequences of our actions, there are also implications for people around us and society.

How to make the right choices

So, how do you make the right choices? First, you must learn to avoid making impulsive decisions. Most bad decisions were made on impulse. Impulsiveness is dangerous as it doesn't take time to consider the consequences of actions.

Actions taken on an impulse usually seek to satisfy the desire for immediate gratification—the need for revenge or pleasure or other self-satisfying endeavors. If you're upset or excited, be calm before taking action. This will save you a lot of pain in the future.

To make the right choices, let's refer to the decision-making process discussed earlier in this chapter. Summarily, consider the choice you want to make. Examine all possible alternatives, including their consequences. You'll have an abundance of stories and personal examples to refer to. By doing so, you can reach a decision that benefits you and those around you.

Taking Responsibility: Accepting Accountability for Decisions and Actions

Sometimes, regardless of how much critical thinking is involved in making a decision, the outcome may not always be pleasant. There's nothing wrong with that. Humanity is limited, so mistakes are possible and always likely.

So, what happens when a decision you made turns out to be wrong? Own up! Yes, take responsibility for your decisions and actions.

Because things go wrong with a particular decision, some people, fearing the consequences, especially in the workplace, tend to shift blame. They may lie about their role in the affair or deflect the blame to someone else to save their head.

Granted, owning up isn't pleasant or palatable, but it is part of your personal growth and has long-term benefits. Let's see how taking responsibility for your actions helps you in the long run.

You learn from your mistakes and become a better person.

Remember the last component of the decision-making process? Yes, reviewing the decision. Reviewing your decision helps you evaluate the outcome of the decision. You can only make an objective review when you take responsibility for your actions.

It helps you see what went wrong and areas you can improve. Learning and relearning are important for self-growth. In the end, even if you made a decision that didn't turn out well, you became a better person out of the process. People who tend to shift blame instead of owning up deny themselves the opportunity to grow because they shut the door to learning.

Another benefit of being accountable for your decisions is that it helps build resilience. You're not only wiser by learning from your mistakes, but you're also stronger.

You gain more control over your life.

Taking responsibility for your actions puts you in greater control of your life. Instead of blaming others and circumstances, when you accept your role in unpleasant outcomes and learn from them, you give yourself greater control over your affairs.

Yes, you made a wrong call, and it didn't turn out right. Now you have learned from it and know how to approach issues better. This line of action gives you more confidence in yourself in the future.

You build trust among your superiors.

When you own up to your actions, your superiors will respect you more. Some people elect to shift blame when their actions lead to unpleasant actions for fear of punishment. This behavior can be counterproductive.

When critical analysis eventually reveals their role in the affair, their superiors or employers will lose trust in them. Taking responsibility will gain your superiors' respect and trust (Bivins, 2006). So, even though things go wrong, they can trust you to be open and honest about anything.

Balancing Values and Priorities

Everyone has values and priorities – a set of important factors, goals, or responsibilities that define our daily lives. Sometimes, our values may be at variance with our priorities. Striking a balance becomes necessary. First, let's define what values and priorities are.

Your values constitute your core beliefs. They determine your worldview, personality, ethics, and decision-making. Your priorities may include your values, but they're a broader term incorporating your personal goals and responsibilities.

Your values and priorities usually work in cohesion. However, as mentioned earlier, depending on the circumstance, they can be at variance. For instance, your values may elevate family over other matters in your life. Still, your specific interests, which help you find meaning, may become too demanding and rob you of quality family time.

At this point, striking a balance becomes important and necessary. While meeting financial obligations is an important priority in your life, your value gives you a sense of fulfillment and contentment.

That's a pretty adult example, but I have a hunch you relate.

Interestingly, when you no longer find fulfillment in life, it can affect your ability to meet other obligations in the first place. Happiness and fulfillment are important drivers in life. More often than not, they're not based on tangible factors like money or possessions.

So, how do you balance your values and priorities? Balancing values and priorities may require self-evaluation. If, at some point in your life, you feel overwhelmed such that you no longer find fulfillment, then something is missing.

Self-evaluation involves identifying your values on one side and your priorities on the other. The next thing is to identify what you can let go. Trade-offs are sometimes necessary to balance values and priorities (Muna & Mansour, 2009).

For instance, if you have a nine-to-five job and love watching soccer, and your family time suffers, you can give up watching soccer for more family time. Of course, recreation is important, but not at the expense of your family.

Alternatively, you can incorporate your values with your priorities. You can watch soccer with your family or find another recreational activity that would interest everyone. This way, your value for family time has blended with your recreation needs.

You can also learn to delegate tasks if your work puts you in a superior role over others. Delegation helps you free up time for more important activities, such as family time.

Avoiding Peer Pressure: Making Independent and Responsible Choices

Everyone belongs to a social group by age, social status, or shared interests (Erikson, 2006). More often than not, these groups tend to influence our actions directly or indirectly. Every human has a basic need for acceptance, especially among peers. This acceptance is usually a function of how much people fit into the interests of their social groups or peers.

Sometimes, the interests of your peers may be at variance with your values. So, it's important to have an independent mind to know when to take a stand for your values when they don't agree with your peers' interests.

Peer pressure is a serious issue in adolescence. Adulthood comes with wisdom, experience, and self-reliance that affords one an independent mind. The need for acceptance is not an important consideration in adulthood as much as in adolescence. This assertion does not imply that peer pressure is no longer a reality in adulthood.

Many teenagers have made terrible choices with devastating consequences because of peer pressure. You must learn to have an independent mind regardless of the trend if you want to overcome peer pressure. Your choices must always be based on your values or convictions and not on the need for acceptance among your peers.

How do you overcome peer pressure? Everything we've discussed so far in this chapter comes to bear on this critical discourse. Overcoming peer pressure is not always easy. It goes beyond just saying no.

Define and protect your values

Remind yourself of your values. Most times, the trend in adolescence and even young adulthood is usually against social values. Knowing what is right and wrong and allowing this knowledge to guide your actions will help you decide where to draw the line. Learn to be firm when you say no and walk away when you should. Your colleagues may mock you on the outside, but they will respect you even though they won't admit it.

Remind yourself of the consequences of choices

If you're struggling with your resolve, it may be necessary to remind yourself of the consequences of the actions you're under pressure to take. This can be all you need to strengthen your resolve against doing something you'll regret.

Change your circle

If you're always in the company of people focused on the wrong things, you may need to change your circle. Link up with people whose values align with yours. This way, peer pressure will give way to collaboration and positive partnerships.

Calculated Decision-Making for Confident Leadership

Confidence and decisiveness in decision-making is an important hallmark of leadership. As a leader, people will rely on you for direction, so you must be ready to make decisions – even unpopular ones – and communicate your choices clearly and effectively. However, many people struggle with decision-making due to a lack of confidence.

You can learn how to make decisions and confidently communicate your decision to others. But before that, let's analyze the reasons for indecisiveness in leadership.

Factors responsible for indecisiveness in leadership

There are a couple of reasons why people are indecisive in making decisions.

The first is **fear**. Fear is a very serious setback for many people. Often, you hear people say, "What if things go wrong?" The fear of failure can make someone go back and forth on a particular decision. The second reason for indecisiveness is a **lack of knowledge**. When you lack sufficient knowledge about a particular issue, you can't trust your decision because you cannot convince others about it. The third reason is **having too much reliance on others**. Some people are too reliant on the opinions of others. They validate their own decisions based on endorsement from others.

At the heart of indecisive leadership is a lack of confidence (Motlung & Lew, 20230). Building self-confidence is, therefore, essential to making strategic decisions for confident leadership.

How to become decisive and confident in decision-making

So, how do you become more confident and gain the trust of others?

Gain more knowledge. Knowledge gives confidence. While you don't have to be an expert on several issues, you should have solid background information on areas where you need to make decisions. Sufficient knowledge helps you make informed decisions and communicate them effectively to others.

Secondly, **consult widely.** Seek advice from experts. You can also ask family and friends where applicable. You'll gain the wisdom to validate your decision and stand by it. Third, p**lan strategically.** Some decisions have long-term implications and so require strategic planning. Keep the big picture in mind while planning so that you can inspire your group to trust in your decisions. The strategies should be feasible, actionable, measurable, and relatable.

Don't be afraid of risks. Leadership is about risk-taking. As a leader, you can't be afraid to make mistakes. Mistakes are part of learning, and they help you gain more valuable experience. When you have made a decision having considered all the factors above, be ready to be accountable for them. Sometimes, we win, sometimes we learn.

Handling Ethical Dilemmas: Navigating Difficult Situations with Integrity

We've noted earlier that ethics are the guiding principles behind the operation of every organization. Ethics preserve organizational ethos while promoting an environment of trust and social cohesion. As a leader, you'll always face difficult decisions with ethical implications.

How you handle these difficulties will cement your credibility. What do you do in these situations? Let's first identify some areas where you may face

Decision-Making and Problem-Solving Strategies

ethical dilemmas as a leader in charge of teams.

One area is in the **allocation of resources**. Sometimes, available resources cannot reach everyone in your group. Who do you reach out to, and who do you leave out?

There could also be **conflicting interests**. Sometimes, you may have to take action against someone close to you in the overall interest of the team.

Decisions about confidentiality issues are also common ethical decisions. Should you protect a whistleblower's identity, or should you expose information that requires urgent action?

How to handle ethical dilemmas

Navigating ethical dimensions is no easy task (Fritzsche, 2000). You'll have to make unpopular decisions and even risk backlash from the teams you lead. The curse of the leader is always having to sacrifice personal comfort and approval in favor of the overall interest.

However, certain principles and actions will guide your decision so that even though they're unpopular, you are confident you made the right decision, which is all that matters anyway.

Remember your values

Your values are central to your actions and may be the only place of comfort when you make an unpopular decision. One value you cannot compromise as a leader is integrity.

Integrity preserves faith in your leadership and your organization. So, for instance, when allocating scarce resources, integrity will make you prioritize merit over relationship.

Advice is golden

Some decisions are not cut-and-dry. They involve gray areas in which either direction may be potentially disastrous. It's important to seek advice at this point. Consult your superiors, mentors, and other leaders. You'll find valuable insight to make the right decisions.

Seeking advice has been mentioned several times in this chapter. It's important at this point to emphasize that a leader should never be tired of consulting other people. A leader requires all the necessary wisdom to handle ethical dilemmas.

Analyze your alternatives

Every potential line of action has its consequences. We've covered this topic earlier in this chapter. Analyze these consequences carefully, considering their merits and demerits. Your interest as a leader should be to protect the overall interest of the organization. See which possible action ensures this goal before making your final decision.

Experience is the best teacher

Unless you're new to leadership, you should be familiar with ethical dilemmas. Although they vary from case to case, you can always draw insight from previous experience. Consider how you handled a previous situation and the outcomes.

Recall that the last component of the decision-making process involves reviewing the actions taken. This review comes in handy when you have to make another decision.

Fostering Honest and Transparent Leadership

It's easy to lead your teams when they trust you. When teams trust their leaders, they are more committed to their duties and more willing to provide open and honest feedback that can help improve productivity.

One of the reasons why your team can trust you is when you're open and honest with them. Although it's not easy to always be open and transparent

Decision-Making and Problem-Solving Strategies

with your team because it can make you vulnerable, the benefits are far-reaching.

What is transparency in leadership?

Transparency in leadership is being open and honest with your team members about your operations, vision, goals, and strategies (Kerfoot, 2004). It also involves letting the teams you lead know how you feel about their performance, including areas where they should. Lastly, it also means owning up and being accountable for your decisions.

Many leaders struggle with transparency because they don't want to appear vulnerable or weak. Interestingly, leadership that places authority over collaboration is stuck in the past and doesn't conform to modern reality.

So, how do you foster honest and transparent leadership? It will be difficult for some people not used to an open culture, but it's a skill that can be learned with time. The ideas below will help you in your journey to becoming a more open and transparent leader.

Be open and honest

If you want to build an honest and transparent work environment, you have to be open and honest. Leaders lead by example. Being honest in all your dealings with your teams will encourage them to follow suit.

Let your teams know where you stand on issues. Communicate your vision, ideas, and strategies as clearly as possible. Be truthful about their performance; commend them or correct them when appropriate and without prejudice. Finally, although it may be difficult, owning up to your mistakes is also important.

Encourage feedback

Encourage your teams always to provide honest feedback about your decisions, strategies, and projects. You must be open to constructive criticism and differing ideas since not everyone will always agree.

By encouraging open communication from your team, you're letting them know you respect their opinions. This will improve their self-confidence and make them more productive in their work.

Involve your team in decision-making

Learn to consult your team members on some important decisions. You'll learn a lot from them, and this information will guide you in further actions. Consulting with your teams will foster a sense of ownership and make them more committed to their work.

Creative Problem-Solving

As a leader, you'll always have problems to solve. Sometimes, some problems may not have conventional solutions, so you'll have to find creative solutions. This process is usually referred to as creative problem-solving.

Creative problem-solving combines divergent and convergent thinking to find the best solution to a problem (Brophy, 1998). In divergent thinking, you generate all potential solutions to a problem, while convergent thinking narrows down these solutions to select the best possible solution.

One limitation of this process is the propensity to make unbalanced or biased decisions, which is inimical to creativity. To address this problem, creative problem-solving involves four principles.

Balanced divergent and convergent thinking

Balancing divergent and convergent thinking is important to promote the creative process.

One way to achieve balance is to use the separate and sequence method. This method advocates a separate time for divergent thinking, where you'll identify all possible solutions to a problem without judgments. You'll need to **be open-minded**. Allow all ideas, regardless of how improbable they may seem. Sometimes, solutions come from the most improbable ideas.

Decision-Making and Problem-Solving Strategies

Also learn to allow feedback. Incorporate feedback from multiple sources during both thinking modes. This would help you gain more insight for better decision-making,

Ask problems as questions

An effective way to seek solutions to problems is to create open-ended questions. Open-ended questions promote creativity by encouraging you to think more critically. In doing so, you can view a situation from multiple perspectives and gain new insights to help problem-solving.

Defer judgment

During divergent thinking, you may be tempted to discard seemingly impossible ideas based on your perspectives. Deferring judgment for a later time allows you to consider all ideas regardless of your personal views.

Use a "yes and" approach to ideas instead of "no, but."

The "Yes and" approach keeps your mind open to possibilities, which is necessary for creativity. When you say "No, but" you stifle creativity by blocking your mind from potential solutions.

The creative problem-solving process.

Although creative problem-solving may not follow conventional thinking, the process involves several cardinal steps: identifying the problem, exploring the ideas, developing solutions, and implementing them.

Defining the problem you want to solve is the first step in creative problem-solving. You can then research the problem to get enough relevant information. Then, formulate questions to help you find solutions or gain more insights. With your crafted questions, you can brainstorm ideas to solve your problem. Divergent thinking takes center stage at this point.

Developing solutions. You now have an abundance of ideas. So, which one is the solution? Employ convergent thinking to narrow down the ideas to one or a few sets of potential solutions. When you settle on a solution, the next thing is to implement it. Before you go ahead, you must create and explain an action plan to your team members.

Collaborative Decision-Making

In making decisions involving teams or groups, you may need to incorporate other team members in your group. This type of decision-making is called collaborative decision-making.

Collaborative decision-making involves collating inputs from other team members and analyzing individual suggestions before deciding. Collaborative decision-making comes with many advantages.

The collaborative decision-making process

Cook (2023) explains how the collaborative decision-making process works and how you can use it to benefit your teams.

First, appoint a facilitator. Choose a member of the group to moderate the process. An ideal facilitator should have sufficient knowledge about the problem at hand. **Next, define the problem.** Clearly identify the problem and its scope. The team members should conduct sufficient research on the issue to gain ample knowledge for a solid foundation for creative thinking.

Next, research potential solutions. Research possible solutions to the problem at hand. Set a yardstick that would help you check whether each solution is feasible. **Then, consider the evidence**. Weigh the pros and cons of each potential solution to help you predict the possible outcomes. **Choose the best alternative**. Use the yardstick you set to select the best alternative after considering the evidence before you.

Advantages of collaborative decision-making

Collaborative decision-making offers numerous advantages.

Decision-Making and Problem-Solving Strategies

It helps you make better decisions. When you pool ideas from other group members, you're more likely to make better decisions. Different personalities in a group will have diverse opinions, offering you a more expanded view of the issue in question. This offers you more knowledge on the subject matter and a greater chance of making the right call.

It also promotes transparency among team members. Collaborating with your teams on important matters promotes open communication and transparency. Your team members will be more willing to provide honest feedback where necessary in such a working environment.

It enhances **mutual respect and trust.** You gain the trust and respect of your team members when you incorporate them into decision-making. The reason is simple: consulting them on important issues means you value their opinions. Apart from an increased willingness to communicate, your team members will be more amenable to taking risks.

Disadvantages of collaborative decision-making

However, collaborative decision-making has some challenges.

Collaborative decision-making can be time-consuming. Sometimes, some situations need urgent responses, requiring you to make swift decisions. Collaboration in this situation may take time and have adverse consequences. **Collaborative decision-making can also lead to conflicts.** Some suggestions may be motivated by personal interests. Such contributions can set the tone for conflicts with other group members.

In all, collaborative decision-making helps you make better decisions by combining and analyzing individual ideas from a group. It offers the advantage of a broader perspective due to the diversity of personalities within a group. However, it's not possible to involve your team in all decisions. Some problems require urgent decisions, and collaboration can do more harm than good in such circumstances.

Workbook 4

1. You and your friend go to the local supermarket to buy some stuff for your school project. You catch your friend shoplifting a headset. You try convincing him to drop it, but he won't. How would you address this issue?
2. You're a student with a part-time job that helps cover your expenses, but it takes up a huge chunk of your study time. How would you balance your need for income with your studies?
3. Think about when your friends want to go to a party after school, but you're unsure if you want to go. They're pushing you to come even though you have other things to do. Write three reasons why you might want to go to the party. Then, write three ways you could deal with their pressure and decide what's right for you.

Takeaway 4

This chapter examined various concepts in decision-making and problem-solving. Leaders always encounter problems that require important decisions. Because decisions may have far-reaching implications, leaders must carefully think through decisions before implementing them. Some decisions may have ethical considerations, in which case the leader must weigh these decisions on the scale of ethical standards, including his own personal values to ensure truth, fairness, and judgment. Some problems will defy conventional solutions, in which case adopting creative problem-solving will help the leader find creative solutions where conventional solutions are not applicable. This process is much easier with the collaborative efforts of your team members

Chapter 5

Team Building and Collaboration

"Great things in business are never done by one person. They're done by a team of people."
– Steve Jobs

Understanding Team Dynamics

Organizations depend on people to drive their vision, each member having a different and clearly defined role. All roles are important, as shortcomings in one role will hamper the group's overall success. Therefore, individuals must work together to support the organization for collective success.

The success of an organization depends on how its team members collaborate in the course of their work. Therefore, for teams to succeed, they must pay attention to team dynamics.

What is team dynamics?

A standard football team has eleven players. Each player has a different position with a different role. The goalkeeper and the defenders must protect the goalposts so the opposing team does not get the ball into the net. At the same time, the midfielders will play to get the ball through to the attackers, whose role is to get the ball into the opposition's goal.

No matter how good the attackers are, they need the ball from the midfielders to attack the opponent's defense. And if the attacker scores as many goals as possible, the goalkeeper must defend the goalposts to keep the scoreline in his team's favor.

The above analogy illustrates how team members must work together to achieve a common goal. How they relate or work together is team dynamics.

Team dynamics may be negative or positive. Positive team dynamics imply that the relationship and cohesion between team members are helping the team achieve its goals. The reverse is the case. Negative team dynamics refers to a situation where the lack of cohesion between team members negatively impacts the organization.

Why is team dynamics so important?

If you want your group project or organization to grow, the teams driving its vision must work cohesively to achieve its goals. Therefore, your success depends on the team dynamics.

Recent data indicates that team collaboration improves individual and team performance (Boskamp, 2023). When team performance improves, the output is always upward.

On the other hand, negative team dynamics impede organizational growth. When teams don't work well together, overall performance is poor, leading to poor output. This brings us to the all-important question: how do you enhance team dynamics?

Managers are the focal point of every team operation. Since performance is top-down, teams generally reflect the strengths and weaknesses of their leaders. As a matter of fact, negative team dynamics are an indirect verdict on the leader's ability to galvanize his team.

Starting with yourself

Look inwards

Any changes to improve team dynamics must begin with the team leader. If your team's performance is subpar, your assessment must begin with you. Evaluate your strengths and weaknesses and identify areas that need improvement.

Team Building and Collaboration

An honest self-appraisal presents an opportunity for personal growth. Identifying areas to improve will help you decide on the required changes. These changes, although necessary, may not be easy. So, there are other things you can do to help you on your self-improvement journey.

Get mentorship

We already said this in part 2, but it's worth mentioning again. When you're part of something bigger than you, especially as a leader, consult people with experience and expertise in your field. The insights and knowledge from your interaction with them will prove valuable to you.

Strategies for your team

While you are working to improve your competence as a leader, your team shouldn't be left out. There are a few ideas for strengthening team cohesion and improving team dynamics.

Communication is central to team dynamics (Moment & Gourgues, 2020). Lack of communication can affect how your team members interact with you and others. Learn to communicate your plans and strategies more clearly and encourage honest feedback.

Put conflicts in perspective. Understand that conflicts are part of the process. So embrace them and ensure your team members don't take them personally. You can also **adopt collaborative decision-making**: Collaborative decision-making enhances team cohesion. Involving your team members in decision-making gives them a sense of belonging and makes them more committed to their duties.

Leading by Example

India was under British rule for almost 90 years, from 1858 to 1947. The British government implemented many unpopular policies against the people during the period. Indian leader Mahatma Gandhi rose to prominence during this era for his advocacy of nonviolent resistance. Gandhi believed in forcing policy changes through nonviolent means of civil resistance.

One of the most unpopular policies of British colonial rule in India was the salt tax (Rather, 2022). The policy meant that only the British government could produce and sell salt. As a result, salt was very expensive, and people with low incomes couldn't afford it.

In March 1930, Gandhi led a protest against this notorious policy, walking 240 miles to the Arabian Sea. This journey took 24 days. Gandhi didn't just voice his concerns against the policy; he walked with fellow protesters to demonstrate their aversion to unjust laws.

By leading from the front, Gandhi inspired others to join the protest without forcing them. Gandhi continues to be known today as the father of nonviolent resistance.

Leading by example is very effective because you're not just telling your team what to do but also showing them how to do it.

What does it mean to lead by example?

Leading by example means you're not just dictating actions for your team to implement but also getting involved. It means you're not afraid to take risks but also ready to be accountable for your actions.

Leading by example shows that you believe in what you're asking your team members to do. It also means that you value your team members and their efforts and are ready to invest your energy for the group's collective success.

The merits of leading by example

Leading by example offers many benefits for you and your team. Leaders who show the way have the trust and confidence of their followers. It makes it easy for them to buy into their vision. By leading by example, you set the standard of excellence. Your team members know what you expect from them. Finally, leading by example improves loyalty and retention.

Building High-Performance Teams

I'm not sure you like football. I love it. I'm into it. Please indulge me because I have to use this next example.

One of the most expensive transfers in British football history is the transfer of Jack Grealish from Aston Villa to Manchester City for 100 million pounds in 2021. Jack Grealish had been the key player at Aston Villa for many years. He was regarded as one of the best midfielders in English football.

However, although Aston Villa was ready to offer him a more lucrative contract, Jack Grealish decided to move to Manchester City. The reason for Jack's decision was not far-fetched. Manchester City were one of the best teams in the world. They had just won the Premier League title and were the most successful English side for the past five seasons.

Jack Grealish made the right decision. That year, Manchester City retained the English Premier League title. Jack Grealish finally had a winner's medal, which eluded him at Aston Villa.

Under Spanish coach Pep Guardiola, Manchester City had become a ruthless force. The reason? He had transformed them into a high-performing team made up of a group of excellent football players.

High-performing teams are highly motivated and have a high propensity for success. We'll see how leaders can build a high-performance team, but first, let's define a high-performance team.

Defining a high-performance team

A high-performance team is a team that is consistently keen on excellence (Aldag & Kuzuhara, 2015). They judge their performance by the highest standards, seeking to raise the bar further. Because life is a constantly changing circus, high-performance teams also maintain excellence by committing to growth and constantly seeking opportunities for personal development.

High-performance teams achieve excellence by setting clear goals, with well-defined roles for each member, communicating frequently, and collaborating effectively.

So, how do you build a high-performance team?

Set the standard. Let your teams know the standard of performance you require from them. Always refer to industry leaders or pacesetters for inspiration. Also, **encourage communication.** High-performance teams are always communicating about everything and anything relevant to their work. To build a high-performance team, encourage communication among your team. Create an environment where your team members can be open and honest with you – the leader – and themselves.

Setting SMART goals will also help you improve team dynamics. If you want to build a high-performance team, you need to set a value system that helps your team achieve their goals. An example of such a value system is the SMART goals. Smart goals are **specific, measurable, achievable, realistic,** and **time-bounding.** Smart goals help benefit your team by reducing stress, saving time, and optimizing performance.

Embracing Diversity in Teams: Leveraging Differences for Collective Success

A glaring reality we face every day as we interact with people is that we're not all the same. Physical differences like gender and race are easy to spot, but our differences are even more profound in intangible things – culture, perspectives, and orientation.

These differences should not alarm you. You can leverage them to build better and more efficient teams by fostering an inclusive environment incorporating ideas, perspectives, and patterns from different people in your organization.

How does diversity and inclusion help in building better and more successful teams?

Benefits of diversity and inclusion

Since 2014, tech companies have spent more than $1.2 billion to promote diversity in their organizations (Alfrey, 2022). Top tech firms like Facebook and Apple have created units for diversity and inclusion with the mandate to create and implement strategies to enhance inclusion in their organizations.

This trend indicates that organizations have identified the numerous benefits of an inclusive culture in a working environment. Not only that, they're also willing to leverage these benefits to drive more success.

So, what are the benefits of a more diverse and inclusive workplace? Embracing diversity and inclusion benefits teams in several ways.

Diversity helps the team make better decisions. When you incorporate ideas from people with different backgrounds and experiences, you expose yourself to different perspectives. This helps you make more informed decisions. It also **promotes creativity and innovation.** Different perspectives mean different ways of solving problems. The effect is enhanced creativity and innovation.

Inclusive teams attract more talents. An inclusive working environment allows people to express themselves without prejudice. Such an environment will attract more people, expanding the talent pool of your team. Also, **inclusive teams offer better customer experience.** An inclusive team is better equipped to cater to the needs of your clients or customers from different backgrounds.

These advantages will make your team more innovative, creative, and productive. So, how do you promote diversity and inclusion in your workplace?

How to promote diversity and inclusion

Start by promoting a culture of inclusion. Let your recruitment pattern show your willingness to create a team of people from diverse backgrounds. Show respect for all cultures. **Discourage discrimination**. Enforce a zero-tolerance policy on discrimination. Ensure that mutual respect and understanding are strongly upheld within your ranks.

Encourage collaboration. Incorporate ideas from all members of your team, irrespective of their differences. Invite them to participate in decision-making, allowing them a sense of belonging. **Show transparency**. Ensure that the same benefits apply to everyone regardless of cultural inclinations and allow everyone equal opportunities.

Finally, lead by example. Let your policies, actions, and body language reflect your commitment to inclusion in your work or business environment. It will be easier to get your team to follow suit.

The Power of Delegation

In 1997, Steve Jobs returned to Apple, the company he had co-founded at a young age. An internal crisis led to his departure in 1985. However, when he returned in 1997, the company's fortunes had nose-dived, and it was on the brink (Elkind, 2008).

Steve Jobs revived Apple in remarkable fashion, restoring the brand's fortune and making it a global leader. When Jobs passed in 2011, Apple had become the world's most valuable brand, valued at $153 billion (Caulfield, 2011).

Jobs built a strong and effective team at Apple by learning to delegate. In his earlier years, before he first left Apple, Jobs tended to be involved in nearly every aspect of the business. This micromanaging behavior proved time-consuming, often creating bottlenecks that stifled progress.

However, in his second tenure, Jobs learned to assign responsibilities to competent individuals, giving them the latitude to express themselves for the collective growth of the organization. The rest is history.

Jobs' success story at Apple underscores the importance of delegation in leadership. Delegation offers numerous benefits, which we shall discuss in the coming sections. We will also understand why some people struggle with delegation and how they can overcome these fears.

What is delegation?

When leaders delegate, they allocate or assign tasks, responsibilities, and decision-making power to a subordinate whose skills and competencies match the role.

As organizations grow, new roles emerge to account for their growing needs. This development makes it more difficult for the leader to be involved in every business process. Doing so can be stressful, time-consuming, and counterproductive. While the leader is bound to suffer a work-life imbalance, other organizational roles will also suffer.

Delegation solves these problems by allowing competent hands to undertake roles while the leader retains a supervisory role. Therefore, the leader can focus on making major policy decisions while enabling team members to implement these decisions.

Elements of delegation

Delegation is characterized by several important elements: trust, communication, authority and responsibility, and accountability.

Leaders can only assign tasks to people they trust. There has to be trust in the ability to deliver on assignments with excellence and on schedule. In assigning roles and responsibilities, leaders must communicate clearly about the expectations for the role and provide necessary guidance.

Assigning roles to individuals also empowers them to make decisions within a well-defined scope, where they become responsible for the outcomes. When individuals receive assignments from their leader, they are accountable to them. The leader, in turn, monitors progress and offers guidance where necessary.

Benefits of delegation

Delegation offers many benefits for both the leader and his team. By assigning tasks to different people, you can have more time to focus on building your brand. With many people in charge of different roles, you can expect greater output.

Delegation reduces your workload, ensuring you have less stress. This has positive implications for your health and well-being. No part of your life suffers when you delegate tasks, ensuring a healthy work-life balance.

Why some people are afraid to delegate

If delegation presents so many benefits, why do some people still struggle with it? In other cases, even after assigning roles, some don't allow their employees enough room to implement their ideas.

One major reason for this behavior is fear. Building a business or organization involves a lot of effort, sacrifices, and investment. Sometimes, one bad decision can take back years of growth. To prevent this, business leaders decide to handle certain aspects of the business themselves.

Regardless of these misgivings, delegation is still a much better alternative to micromanagement. Leaders can overcome this fear by assigning tasks only to competent persons suited for such roles. Competence builds trust, which is an essential component of delegation.

Communication is also key. The leader must clearly explain the role's requirements and other related parameters. Constant communication helps the leader provide guidance while tracking individual progress.

Conflict Management in Teams

In 2018, leaked documents revealed that social media giant Facebook was embroiled in an internal conflict, pitching employees against the management. Some employees were concerned that Russian operatives used the platform to spread misinformation about the 2016 US Presidential Election.

Although the magnitude of the effect of the fake news on the outcome of the election could not be determined, there was a strong perception that it had caused a substantial shift in public opinion.

Some Facebook employees believed the company could have done more to moderate content being shared on its platform (Esberg, 2021). Meanwhile, another group of employees disagreed. This group believed that such actions would be synonymous with politically biased censorship.

These disagreements led to serious debates within the rank and file of Facebook. The reality of this conflict became known after leaked documents entered the public domain. Facebook eventually responded by taking some measures to curb the spread of fake news using fact-checking mechanisms.

These kinds of conflicts are not strange, especially in teams with diverse cultures and backgrounds. As a leader, you'll need conflict management skills to quell internal tensions and find solutions to drive your team forward.

This section will discuss the concept of conflict management and explain how you can use it to improve team productivity. You'll also learn the different skills required for conflict management.

What is conflict management?

Conflict management is a system of actions involved in resolving conflicts, disputes, and disagreements with a group. Conflict management aims to find a common ground that protects the interests of all parties involved.

Conflicts are inevitable. As teams work together to achieve a common goal, individuals will approach their tasks according to their peculiar personalities. Consequently, there's bound to be a clash of opinions, ideas, perspectives, and interests.

These clashes can escalate into a crisis if not managed properly. Conflicts can create a toxic environment, damaging productivity and eventually derailing a team's progress. A leader must, therefore, act swiftly and restore order and harmony.

Conflict management moves beyond resolving disputes. It also seeks to leverage understanding of the causative issues to build a stronger and more motivated team.

What causes conflicts?

Conflicts may take different forms, but the same number of factors usually cause them. The following issues are usually the major causes of conflicts in a group.

- **Personality clashes**: The different members of your team will have different perspectives on issues and different approaches to work, which can lead to friction.

- **Inadequate communication**: Lack of communication can lead to misunderstanding and misrepresentation, a potential cause of conflict.

- **Resource allocation**: Competition for scarce resources in a group can put individual members against one another.

- **Ambiguity of roles**: Failure to clearly define roles can lead to confusion and clash of interests.

- **Lack of fairness**: Undue favoritism or undue aggression toward a particular person in a group can lead to resentment.

- **Workload imbalance**: Tensions can arise when one person or a group takes a greater share of the overall burden and doesn't get adequate compensation.

Conflict management skills

Good leaders are excellent conflict managers. They understand the nature of conflicts to escalate with serious consequences. So, they swiftly move to reduce tensions and resolve conflicts. Leaders must have the following skills to manage conflicts in the workplace adequately.

- **Empathy**: Leaders must show concern and understanding of how issues may have caused emotional distress to a person or group of persons within a group.
- **Communication**: Leaders must communicate clearly to manage conflicts while encouraging open dialogue.
- **Compromise**: Conflicts can only be resolved when the contending parties' concerns are addressed so that everyone wins. Most times, it requires shifting of grounds.

How to manage conflicts

When conflicts arise, the first step is to understand the issues behind the conflict. This involves honest and open dialogue. The leader encourages everyone involved to express their misgivings by opening communication lines. This allows the leader to identify the issues behind the conflict.

After identifying the issues, the leader may also allow suggestions from the contending parties on the way forward. Everyone wants to end the conflict in a way that addresses their concerns. These suggestions help the leader identify possible solutions to the conflict.

The next step is to carefully analyze each potential solution and decide on the best option. The best solutions often involve compromises, where parties have to shift grounds to accommodate everyone's interests.

Encouraging Innovation

The Post-it Note is one of the world's most widely used stationery products. It helps people jot down ideas, tasks, and information and stick them to areas within reach for easy reference.

Although widely used, only a few people know how the Post-it notes existed. The invention of this revolutionary product is credited to Dr. Spencer Silver, a scientist who was working at 3M, a company known for making innovative products (Nayak et al., 1997).

Back in 1968, Spencer stumbled on an adhesive that could stick to surfaces and be easily removed without leaving any residue. Spencer thought of practical ways to apply this discovery and informed the company of his discovery.

It wasn't until four years later that one of his colleagues, Art Fry, found a use for it. The bookmarks Fry used for his hymnal during a seminar kept falling out. The frustration led to the realization of the need for a non-destructive and easily removable adhesive like the one Spencer had discovered years ago.

Fry collaborated with Spencer to develop the Post-it Note by applying the adhesive to small pieces of yellow paper. Although there was an initial lack of support from 3M due to skepticism about its practicality and commercial potential, Spencer and Fry's persistence saw to the product's success that revolutionized office management.

The inspiring account above illustrates how innovation can transform aspects of our daily lives. The impact of innovation is evident in every aspect of human endeavor – medicine, education, media, etc. The list is endless.

It, therefore, becomes essential for leaders to encourage innovation in the workplace. Who knows where the next big idea will come from? This section highlights the benefits of innovation, identifies common barriers to innovation, and provides valuable insights on how to encourage innovation in the workplace.

Why you should encourage innovation in the workplace

Apart from solving problems and engineering social change, innovation in the workplace offers many potential benefits.

It gives you a competitive advantage. In today's highly competitive environment, innovation helps you stay ahead. Innovation also **improves efficiency**: By encouraging innovation, your employees can design and create new processes that improve your business operations.

Constantly improving your products through innovation will keep your customers happy and improve customer retention. **It will also increase talent attraction**. An environment that encourages innovation is a haven for talented individuals. **Finally, it improves brand appeal**. The benefits that come with innovation will significantly improve your brand's value.

What hinders innovation?

Innovation thrives under a supportive environment. The lack of support and other impact factors can hinder productivity. Let's discuss some of these factors.

Lack of diversity

A team that lacks diversity will not benefit from the promise of creativity that a more inclusive culture provides. Homogeneous teams usually think alike and are likely to remain stuck in the same ways of doing things.

Complacency

If you're satisfied with the current realities around you, you won't be open to new possibilities. Complacent leaders and their teams do not actively seek opportunities for improvement.

Resistance to change

When leaders are stuck on tradition, they're averse to programs or ideas that can cause them to adjust to a new culture. This behavior stifles creativity and innovation.

Fear of failure

The fear of failure prevents some leaders from supporting ideas that may seem outlandish. Lack of support kills the energy behind the ideas, as an individual may be unable to drive the process.

Lack of resources

Driving an innovative process can be expensive. Therefore, a lack of funding and other essential resources can pose a significant roadblock in the eventual success of an innovative idea.

How to encourage innovation

The suggestions below will help encourage innovation in your workplace.

First**, have an open mind**. An open mind is receptive to new possibilities, no matter how improbable. Second, **be willing to take risks**: Because innovation may require significant investment, some leaders are afraid to commit to ideas they may not find convincing.

Thirdly, **prioritize creativity.** Let your employees know you value creativity and are ready to support creative ideas. Fourth, **support and reward innovation**. Being receptive to new ideas is not sufficient without the necessary support. You must learn to commit both financially and otherwise to innovation. Finally, **allow autonomy**. Allowing your employees to explore and act on ideas will enhance creativity. A creative working environment is a breeding ground for innovation.

Developing Leadership in Peers

Keynote speaker and thought leader on peer advantage Leo Bottary (2014) gave an interesting account of how his four-year-old daughter demonstrated peer leadership.

The story goes that he had gone to pick her up after a Halloween party at a childcare center. When he arrived, the woman at the desk informed Leo that the childcare center director would love to see him.

Worried that something might be wrong, he entered the director's office. The director of the center narrated to Leo how his little daughter was able to address the fears of her peers.

So, the center had brought a "witch" to entertain the children for the Halloween party. However, this move turned out to be a bad idea.

The witch appeared real, scaring the kids, who began to cry. Although the teachers tried to reassure the children that the witch wasn't real and they were safe, the kids were not convinced, so the crying did not stop.

Fortunately, there was a moment of respite when Leo's daughter got up from where she sat at the front of the class. Standing before her peers, she waved her hands in the air and shouted, 'She's not real!" At this point, the kids stopped crying and calm returned to the room.

What is leadership in peers?

Leadership by peers simply means the ability to lead and influence a group of people on the same level or status as you. Leading your peers is a bit more complex than our traditional leadership.

In traditional leadership, the leader has legitimate authority to enforce standards, rule, and determine the team's direction. This authority is absent in peer leadership. Although leadership generally requires skills to be effective, authority bestows more advantages on traditional leadership.

The important question, therefore, becomes how peer leaders can inspire and lead their group effectively.

Without the advantage of legitimate authority, peer leadership requires skill and tact to influence people on the same level as you.

The absence of legitimate authority in peer leadership may seem to be a disadvantage. However, this disadvantage presents a huge opportunity for influencing real change based on respect, loyalty, and admiration. Such influence can yield more effective results.

How to develop leadership in peers

You'll need to learn the following to inspire loyalty and influence your peers.

Exemplary leadership

When you demonstrate the values you demand from your peers, you gain their trust and respect. Whether they're peers or not, people naturally respect people they can trust.

Taking Initiative

Being proactive in decision-making and problem-solving will get your peers to respect you. You'll become a rallying point for people not confident enough to make decisions.

Knowledge

If you're the most knowledgeable person in a group, they'll likely consult you on several issues. Gain knowledge by reading and taking relevant courses.

Effective communication

The ability to clearly express your thoughts and ideas respectfully will earn your peers' admiration.

Conflict resolution

Taking active steps to resolve conflicts among your team members will make them respect you.

Leading peers may not be easy, but when you earn the trust and respect of your peers, you'll have little trouble leading and inspiring them for collective success.

Recognizing and Appreciating Contributions to Team Achievements

Amazon employee Rajat Shah could not contain his excitement. Shah (2020) narrates the surreal feeling of receiving the annual Amazon "Just Do It Award" from CEO Jeff Bezos in October 2020.

Shah was the brain behind Amazon's Gather, a platform that allows people to meet virtually from any part of the world. This platform was particularly useful during the COVID-19 pandemic when governments around the globe had placed restrictions on movement to curb the spread of the disease.

Every year, the "Just Do It" Award recognizes two selected employees whose contributions demonstrated the company's core values of innovation and bias for action. This award is part of the company's efforts to recognize and appreciate contributions to team achievements.

Recognition and appreciation, just like the Amazon awards, is one way to keep your team members motivated. You may not need to hold an elaborate annual event like Amazon to appreciate your team members, but you can create a culture of recognition in your team.

You can incorporate several ideas in your work culture to show your employees that you appreciate their contributions to your company's success. This section discusses these ideas and provides insights on how you can introduce them.

Ways to recognize and appreciate your team

On-the-spot commendations

While you wait for the big stage like Amazon's Just Do It award, you can commend your team members on the spot when the opportunity arises.

Emails and Calls

Sending emails is another way to recognize and appreciate your team. In your email, explain their contributions and how they contributed to team success. You can also call them on the phone and let them know how much you value your contributions.

Public recognitions

Your team members will also appreciate public recognition like the Amazon Just Do It awards. Whatever you do, the key idea is to ensure that your strategies for recognising and appreciating your team align with their preferences and your own values.

Workbook 5

1. Your teacher comes from Africa where students don't use first names for teachers. Some classmates make fun of him by using his first name meanly. You know he won't react because things are different here. But you're unhappy about the disrespect. How would you talk to your classmates to help them understand and be more sensitive and receptive to cultural differences?

2. Your teacher isn't here today, and your classmates are getting noisy and disorganized. Assume you're the leader now. Write down what you would do to help the class stay calm, interested, and working well until the teacher returns.

4. In your school laboratory project, you and your classmates are divided on using distilled or tap water to rinse the lab equipment. This has caused some tension within the team. How would you handle this disagreement to maintain positive team dynamics and ensure a successful project outcome?

Takeaway 5

This chapter examined the concept of team collaboration and its implications for the success of any organization. It explored important concepts like team dynamics, exemplary leadership, conflict management, high-performance teams, delegation, innovation, peer leadership, and having a reward system. The discourse provided valuable insights into how leaders can enhance team motivation and productivity by promoting collaboration, resolving conflicts, and building confidence through delegation and rewards

Chapter 6

Overcoming Fear and Embracing Change

"Everything you want is on the other side of fear."
- Jack Canfield

Understanding Fear

During his time as a political prisoner, Mandela faced numerous fears. He spent 27 years in prison for his anti-apartheid activism in South Africa. However, instead of letting fear dominate him, Mandela confronted and understood his fears.

While in prison, he developed a deep understanding of fear as a tool of oppression and control (Ofili, 2018). He once wrote, "I learned that courage was not the absence of fear, but the triumph over it." Mandela's ability to analyze and comprehend fear allowed him to maintain his resilience, keep his spirit alive, and ultimately contribute to dismantling apartheid.

Mandela's story underscores the importance of understanding fear and transforming it into a driving force for change. His ability to face fear head-on and use it as a catalyst for positive action demonstrates how a deeper understanding of our fears can empower us to overcome them and significantly impact the world.

To understand fear, we need the right knowledge. This section provides an adequate knowledge of fear. It examines the concept of fear, highlights the causes, and identifies the symptoms. It also provides valuable suggestions for coping with fear.

What is fear?

Humans love comfort and security. We always react to any real or perceived threats to our sense of security. Fear is the sudden rush of emotion we feel when we find ourselves in positions or situations that seem to dent our sense of security.

Fear can manifest in different ways. But before we get to that, let's first identify the different causes of fear.

What causes fear?

Several factors can trigger fear. They may be real or imagined. Whether real or imagined, these factors puncture our sense of security and make us anxious.

Fear can be caused by

What are the symptoms of fear?

When your body senses fear, it responds in certain ways. This response manifests in physical, emotional, cognitive, and behavioral changes to the degree of intensity of the fear.

Common physical changes include rapid breathing, sweating, increased heartbeat, and muscle tension. Emotional responses include anxiety, feelings of doom, and pain.

Cognitive responses include loss of concentration, wandering thoughts, and feelings of being overwhelmed. We respond in our behavior by seeking reassurances or seeking safety, or moving or running away from the objects of fear.

Types of fear

The common types of fear humans face include phobia, social anxiety, generalized anxiety disorder, panic attacks, and fear of failure.

Persons with phobia manifest symptoms of fear when they see certain objects or find themselves in certain situations. **Social anxiety makes some** people avoid social situations for fear of being judged or embarrassed. Generalized anxiety disorder refers to constant and persistent worry over general life issues. They can have physical manifestations of fear.

Panic attack refers to intense and sudden fear, which is usually accompanied by shortness of breath and rapid heartbeat. **Fear of failure** describes a situation where people avoid failing to meet expectations; some people avoid taking up responsibilities and challenges.

Other types include fear of change and fear of rejection. In any case, we usually respond to fears by avoiding situations that trigger such emotions.

The most common social fear is fear of failure. It prevents many people from making progress in life. Because making progress involves risk-taking, people who have a fear of failure avoid taking these risks.

Overcoming Fear of Failure

Renowned inventor Thomas Edison is known for his incredible persistence and his willingness to learn from failure. While working on creating the electric light bulb, he faced numerous setbacks and encountered over a thousand failed attempts. Despite these challenges, Edison viewed each failure as a valuable learning experience.

He famously said, "I have not failed. I've just found 10,000 ways that won't work." Edison's attitude toward failure was instrumental in his success. He understood that failure is not a final outcome but a stepping stone toward success.

Overcoming Fear and Embracing Change

Ultimately, Edison's perseverance paid off. He eventually developed a practical and commercially viable incandescent light bulb, revolutionizing the world of technology and lighting. His story is an inspiring example of how embracing failure and using it as a stepping stone can lead to groundbreaking achievements.

Like Thomas Edison's, numerous stories abound of people who overcame their fears, achieving great feats. This section provides practical steps on how to overcome the fear of failure.

How to overcome the fear of failure

Erin Eatough (2022), in a post on BetterUp, offers some practical steps for overcoming fear, which we shall discuss now.

Failure is normal.

Erin believes that accepting failure as a part of life would help you overcome the fear of failure. No one wants to fail. However, we can always find lessons in our mistakes and use these lessons to our advantage.

Failure is not the end of the world. When we fail, we give ourselves the opportunity to learn. This knowledge would be valuable in our next endeavor.

Talk to someone

Erin believes that talking to someone can lighten your fears and help you see things differently. You can talk to a friend, a family member, or even see a therapist.

Consider the options.

The fear of failure often keeps you fixated on just the negative outcome of an action. However, it can help you to consider other possibilities.

Not trying at all is a bigger disaster.

While there are many possibilities to giving it a try, not trying at all shuts you out completely to any chance of success. You might end up regretting this lack of action much later in life.

Make changes on the way.

Life is not static, so you can make changes along the way as you embark on your journey. People quit jobs, change careers, or extend deadlines they have fixed for themselves.

Take the challenge head-on.

Erin admits that your fears may never go away, but it doesn't mean you shouldn't try. It's okay to fear, but don't allow your fears to control you and limit your experiences in life.

Cultivating Courage

I remember watching Malala address the United Nations a couple of years ago. It was inspiring to see such a young girl from Pakistan speak to the world about her advocacy for the education of the girl child.

Yes, Malala was the poster girl of female child education. But something else brought her to the limelight: her courage.

Malala Yousafzai demonstrated exceptional courage in adversity (Livingstone et al., 2012). In 2012, at the age of 15, she was targeted by the Taliban for advocating girls' education in her home region of Swat Valley.

Despite receiving threats and surviving an assassination attempt, Malala continued to speak out for girls' rights to receive an education.

Her determination and bravery inspired people worldwide and led to her being awarded the Nobel Peace Prize in 2014, making her the youngest-ever Nobel laureate.

Overcoming Fear and Embracing Change

Malala's story demonstrates how courage can lead to positive change and impact, even in the most challenging and dangerous circumstances.

Challenges are everywhere, at home, school, or in the business place – there's never a shortage of challenges.

However, if we learn to face our challenges head-on, endless possibilities await us. So how do you learn to cultivate courage? This section provides some practical insights.

Ways to cultivate courage

1. Face your fears.

At some point, you would have to accept that the challenges will not go away. So you'll have to take them head-on. Being courageous is like training in the gym. The more you flex your muscles, the less terrifying the challenges appear.

2. Be optimistic.

As mentioned earlier, fear makes you focus only on the negative outcomes, blinding you to the numerous exciting possibilities of a course of action. Instead of focusing on what could go wrong, encourage yourself with positive possibilities.

3. Practice self-care.

Several self-care techniques can help you relax and feel less anxious about your fears. You could practice yoga, meditation, mindfulness, and hypnosis to release the tension and unburden yourself.

Whatever you do, keep in mind that the decision to face your fears is the beginning of an exciting journey in your life. Fear can limit you, but courage can liberate you!

Facing Social Anxiety

American comedian and actress Andrea Savage has used different mediums to discuss her struggles with social anxiety.

Savage's story is relatable to many who face social anxiety. Despite her comedy career, she admitted to feeling anxious in social situations and fearing public speaking.

She worked to overcome her anxiety by seeking therapy, practicing mindfulness techniques, and gradually exposing herself to situations that triggered her anxiety.

Through her journey, Savage found ways to manage her social anxiety and used her experiences as material for her comedy.

Her story highlights how individuals can work through their fears, seek help, and even find ways to turn their challenges into sources of strength and creativity.

Like Savage, social anxiety affects millions around the world. Sadly, most people respond by running away from situations that trigger anxiety. This section provides practical insights on how you can deal with social anxiety.

What is social anxiety?

Social anxiety is the fear of being in social situations (Morrison et al., 2013). People with social anxiety are afraid of being judged, embarrassed, or humiliated. As a result, they tend to avoid being in social settings that require them to speak or contribute to social activities.

By causing an individual to avoid social settings, social anxiety can rob them of experiences that can enrich their lives.

What causes social anxiety?

Social anxiety can result from many factors, such as trauma, genetics, environmental factors, past experiences, personality traits, and even changes in brain chemistry.

How do you deal with social anxiety?

The following tips can help you overcome social anxiety and become the star that you are.

Practice exposure therapy.

Remember the analogy of flexing muscles in the gym? You can use the same method to overcome social anxiety. Gradually expose yourself to social settings. Make little contributions and increase them gradually as time goes on.

Eventually, you'll get accustomed to such settings and be less worried about external perception. You may even come to realize that many people are not as judgmental as you think.

Learn social skills.

What if you have social anxiety because you lack confidence in yourself? You can solve this problem by working on your communication skills. Improve your social skills to build your confidence and make you less anxious about making mistakes.

Get a support system.

Sometimes, we could use a little support. Talk to friends, join support groups, or see a therapist. These interactions will help you release tension and gain more insight as you listen to others to address your problem.

Practice self-care.

Practicing self-care can help you relax. In an earlier section, I suggested techniques like meditation, mindfulness, yoga, and hypnosis. These techniques are also useful here, and they will help you a great deal.

Mindfulness and Stress Management

Jon Kabat-Zinn, a professor of medicine, is credited for the rise of mindfulness in mainstream Western medicine. In the late 1970s, he developed the Mindfulness-Based Stress Reduction (MBSR) program, which integrates mindfulness meditation and awareness techniques to help individuals manage stress, pain, and various health conditions.

One of Kabat-Zinn's notable success stories involves a patient named "Bob." Bob had been dealing with chronic pain and faced surgery as a last resort. However, he decided to enroll in the MBSR program before going through with the surgery. Through consistent mindfulness practices, Bob learned to manage his pain and stress, and he decided to forego the surgery altogether.

This experience led to the recognition of the significant impact mindfulness can have on stress reduction and overall well-being. Kabat-Zinn's work and Bob's story demonstrate how mindfulness techniques can empower individuals to better manage stress, pain, and various life challenges, fostering a greater sense of control and resilience.

Like Bob, many people are taking advantage of mindfulness techniques to improve the quality of their lives. This section explains the concept and practice of mindfulness, and you can use it to deal with fear and anxiety.

What is mindfulness?

Mindfulness is a practice that brings you to focus on the present without judgment. Mindfulness helps you pay attention to your thoughts and surroundings. People practice mindfulness alongside other activities like yoga, meditation, and exercise.

Benefits of mindfulness

Bob's story, as we noted earlier, illustrates the therapeutic power of mindfulness. Indeed, mindfulness is a form of healing that can benefit you in several ways.

Mindfulness reduces stress. By helping you relax, mindfulness helps you cope with stress. It helps to **improve mental focus.** Practicing mindfulness regularly helps you learn to concentrate and be more focused on tasks until you finish them.

If you're suffering from insomnia, mindfulness can be a way to improve your sleep. Mindfulness improves your mood, relaxes you, and reduces stress. You'll sleep better as a result. Mindfulness can lead to **improved emotional intelligence.** By helping you become more aware of your emotions, you can learn to react better and avoid impulsive reactions. Mindfulness also **improves self-awareness.** By encouraging self-reflection, mindfulness helps you learn about your thoughts, feelings, and behavior.

How do you practice mindfulness?

You can learn and incorporate several mindfulness techniques into your daily life. These include mindful breathing, body scan, mindful eating, mindful love and kindness, and mindful walking.

To practice mindful breathing, focus your awareness on your thoughts for a few minutes as you breathe in and out without trying to change them. Body scan involves focusing your awareness on a selected body part and observing any sensations without reacting to them.

In mindful eating, you eat slowly while focusing your attention on the sensations of holding, chewing, tasting, smelling, and swallowing the food. **Mindful love and kindness** involve directing positive wishes to yourself, your family, close friends, and the rest of humanity. Mindful walking involves paying attention to your breathing, body movements, and surroundings while walking or rolling.

Mindfulness and stress management

Stress is your body's natural response to fear or anxiety (Robinson, 1990). In response to sudden perceived threats, your body activates its "fight-or-flight mode" in preparation for action. Stress is normal now and then, but excessive or chronic stress can lead to stress disorders.

Mindfulness techniques are an effective method of coping with stress. You can relax, become more self-aware, and cope better with stressors through these techniques.

Developing Adaptability and Flexibility in Leadership

When Nadella took over as CEO of Microsoft in 2014, Microsoft was facing challenges in adapting to the rapidly changing tech landscape. The company was known for its traditional software model, but the industry was shifting toward cloud computing and mobile devices.

Nadella recognized the need for a change in approach. He focused on fostering a culture of innovation, collaboration, and adaptability within the company. Under his leadership, Microsoft shifted its focus toward cloud services like Azure and embraced a more open and collaborative approach with other platforms and technologies.

This shift in strategy required Nadella to be flexible and adaptable in his leadership style. He encouraged employees to take risks, experiment, and learn from failures. His approach led to Microsoft's successful transformation into a cloud-first, mobile-first company, and its market value soared under his leadership.

Satya Nadella's story highlights the importance of adaptability and flexibility in leadership, especially in the face of industry changes. His willingness to embrace new ideas, pivot the company's strategy, and foster a culture of continuous learning has contributed to Microsoft's ongoing success.

Resistance to change can have severe consequences. The story of Nokia and BlackBerry are perfect examples of what can happen to an organization that fails to adapt to changes.

Overcoming Fear and Embracing Change

In their prime, Nokia and BlackBerry were industry leaders in mobile device technology. Nokia was the best-selling Symbian phone in the early 2000s, while BlackBerry was popular for its revolutionary messaging platform and user-friendly keypad devices based on the BlackBerry OS. But Android technology came on board, offering improved consumer experience.

Nokia and BlackBerry counted on their expansive consumer base and stuck to their proprietary software. When realization struck, it was already too late. While Nokia has attempted to win hearts in recent years, nobody remembers BlackBerry anymore.

To remain relevant, leaders must learn to be flexible and willing to embrace change. Life is dynamic. New trends and ideas are emerging every day. As a leader, you must also monitor trends to help your team adapt to new realities.

Change can be scary, especially for those who have been doing the same thing in a particular field of endeavor for a long time. However, learning to adapt also means being open to learning and relearning.

Decades ago, energy companies like Royal Dutch Shell and ExxonMobil were the world's most valuable firms. Today, with an increased campaign for adopting green energy for environmental sustainability, the demand for fossil fuels is dropping.

Electric cars are becoming more popular, with many cities now boasting sufficient charging infrastructure. In fact, many countries have passed laws that make it illegal to use fossil fuels from 2023.

Learning to adapt to new realities in a constantly changing world has become necessary for survival. Like the unfortunate stories of Nokia and BlackBerry, resistance to change can be devastating. Rather like Nadella, be open to change. According to a quote whose author is unknown, change is a necessary pain.

Building Resilience

Life is full of ups and downs. One minute, we're excited; the next, a difficult moment can steal our joy. While we always hope for the best, we can't predict what will happen next.

Nobody has a perfect life, not even the super-rich. The bad days will come. While we don't know its shape, our resolve to life will be tested. The measure of this resolve is resilience.

Resilience is the ability to adapt to setbacks and challenges and bounce back from them. Resilience determines how much inner strength you can draw to keep going in the face of adversity.

Resilience is also the ability to persevere in the face of continuous rejection and setbacks. It's easy to give up or give in, but the ability to continue to push your dreams against the odds can produce astonishing success.

Resilient leaders can motivate their teams to bounce back from failure while continuing to push for success. Teams draw inspiration from their leaders. So, if you want to build a strong, resilient team, the process must begin with you.

How you can build resilience

Resilience doesn't come overnight, but you can develop it with time using the strategies below.

- **Build a strong support system**: Develop positive relationships. By having people around who genuinely care for you, you can find support during difficult times.
- **Stay positive**: Have the mindset that every setback or challenge is temporary and better days are ahead.
- **Learn from rejection**: Look inward to find out why your work or idea was rejected and make improvements.

- **Practice mindfulness**: Mindfulness will help you relax, boost your mood, and give you the energy to bounce back.

The Growth Mindset

In his early years, Michael Jordan faced challenges and setbacks. He was cut from his high school basketball team, which could have discouraged him from pursuing his passion. However, Jordan used this setback as motivation to work even harder. He developed a growth mindset, believing his skills could improve with dedication and effort.

Throughout his career, Jordan's work ethic and determination were unparalleled (Willis, 2023). He consistently practiced, refined his skills, and sought ways to elevate his game. He didn't let failures or setbacks define him; instead, he viewed them as opportunities to learn and grow.

Jordan's growth mindset played a pivotal role in his success. He became one of the greatest basketball players ever, winning multiple championships and accolades. His story highlights the importance of believing in the potential for growth and improvement and how adopting a growth mindset can lead to great success.

What is a growth mindset?

A growth mindset is a way of thinking that believes that ability depends on how hard you work. It is the opposite of a fixed mindset that believes ability is primarily an inborn trait.

As Fran (2023) explains, proponents of a growth mindset are always seeking opportunities to improve and hone their skills. Conversely, people who lean toward a fixed mindset do not see the need for self-improvement as they believe that abilities are inborn and active throughout a person's lifetime.

Having a growth mindset allows you to improve and explore more opportunities for growth and self-development. As a leader, a growth mindset will make you drive your team to constant self-development, opening up more ground for improved productivity.

A fixed mindset doesn't encourage growth and personal development. While some abilities may be inborn, performance is not. Failure to improve them will leave you behind in the scheme of things in a highly competitive and ever-changing world.

How you can develop a growth mindset

The following strategies will help you develop a growth mindset.

Identify your mindset

The first step is to access your own way of thinking. Do you have a growth mindset or a fixed mindset? What is your attitude toward learning and self-improvement? Do you see your abilities as innate or a result of hard work?

Analyze your recent progress

Identify areas where you've improved recently. Consider the changes you made that led you to such progress. What efforts did you make to achieve this? These considerations will reinforce your conviction in the reality of a growth mindset.

Analyze the success of other people

Consider success stories around you. See how the people involved recorded such achievements. Was it a case of pure genius or hard work?

View efforts as a way to develop mastery

Even if skills are inborn, effort helps you become more proficient. As Thomas Edison puts it, "success is one percent genius, and ninety-nine percent perspiration."

Avoid complacency and embrace change

A growth mindset doesn't encourage complacency. Even in success, seek to improve. In a highly competitive world, embracing and adapting to change will give you an advantage.

Cultivating Optimism

Helen Keller was both blind and deaf from a very young age due to an illness. Despite these profound challenges, Keller's determination and optimism guided her through a life of remarkable accomplishments. With the help of her teacher, Anne Sullivan, Keller learned to communicate through touch and developed a deep understanding of language.

Keller's optimism was evident in her perspective on life. She once said, "Although the world is full of suffering, it is also full of the overcoming of it." She focused on her opportunities and abilities rather than dwelling on her limitations.

Keller became an author, political activist, and lecturer, advocating for the rights of people with disabilities and inspiring others with her resilience. Her story showcases the power of cultivating optimism in the face of adversity and how maintaining a positive outlook can lead to personal growth and a lasting impact on the world.

Optimism is the fuel that drives hope in the face of difficulty. Without optimism, a person has no will to live, much less make any effort for personal growth. Optimism is contagious; optimistic leaders can keep their teams motivated even in the face of difficulties. Learn what optimism is and how you can cultivate it.

What is optimism?

Optimism is the quality of having a positive outlook on life. It's the belief in a favorable future even though current realities suggest otherwise. Because optimistic individuals believe that things will generally work out for the better, they approach situations constructively while maintaining resilience.

How you can cultivate optimism

Setbacks will always come, but you need to develop optimism if you can't find the motivation to deal with setbacks and forge ahead. Here are ways in which you can achieve that.

- **Be grateful**: There are positive aspects of your life that you should be grateful for. Identify them and use them to inspire yourself.
- **Focus on problem-solving**: Instead of dwelling on the setback, understand why it happened and how you can find solutions.
- **Set realistic goals**: Always ensure your goals are realistic. Use the SMART yardstick to test whether they would work or not.
- **Avoid negativity**: Stay away from negative people or groups. Like optimism, negativity is also contagious.

Workbook 6

Question 1: Recall a time when you faced a challenging situation, like giving a presentation after a previous mistake. Reflect on how that experience made you feel and how it affected your confidence. Now, imagine you have a friend who is in a similar situation. How would you advise them?

Question 2: Your friend is scared to return to school because of bullying. What advice would you give to help him overcome his fear and feel more confident about returning to school?

Question 3: Your dance team has lost the school competition for two years in a row. This has led to decreasing interest among team members. Brainstorm and write down three creative and motivating ideas to reignite the team's passion and commitment to dance and strategies to improve your chances of winning next year's competition.

Takeaway 6

This chapter explained the meaning of fear. It offered useful insights on how to cope with them. Fear is limiting and can prevent you from taking opportunities that could elevate you. Fear in itself isn't bad; it's a natural human emotion. However, it shouldn't control your life. Courage, resilience, and optimism can help you face and overcome your fears. Mindfulness practice is more of a supportive therapy that helps you come to terms with your fears while helping you relax. It involves several techniques that help you study your thoughts and emotions without any judgments.

Part 2

Leading with Integrity and Impact

Oprah Winfrey tested several unsuccessful iterations on a small local show before defining her leadership style as a unique voice of global impact. Her story mirrors the experience of many global leaders you now admire. They typically tested various platforms and ideas before developing into a brand that influences and leads every other person.

In this book's final part, you'll discover how to create a personal brand that "speaks", while enhancing your leadership image to others. In a world where everyone wants to impress, having a well-defined personal brand can help you create great connections and following.

Without giving in to bullying, low self-esteem, or unhealthy competition, you'll see how to explore social media to grow your unique leadership influence and empower others.

Finally, I'll show you how fortunate your generation is to have globally acclaimed trailblazers who have gained ethical digital influence.

Remember, your mental and emotional health is vital and requires equal attention as empowering others. You don't want to skip any chapter in this part. Each links seamlessly into the other, with actionable tips you can apply to grow your leadership influence immediately.

Chapter 7

Personal Branding and Leadership Image

If you're not branding yourself, you can be sure others will do it for you
– Anonymous

Understanding Personal Branding

Young entrepreneurs and leaders get a little negative public image. Sadly, teens tend to suffer from a closed stereotype from older ones of being lazy, entitled, and obsessively addicted to gadgets.

They fall victim to the narrative that they may not be taken seriously for their youthful age or looks. The stereotype might have some elements of reality to it. But it definitely isn't all the truth.

Many teens globally aren't just thinking (or living) outside that box; some have broken that box to redefine culture with their global brands. They've achieved prominence, and Meta's Mark Zuckerberg is a popular name I hope you don't mind recalling.

Only 19 and a Harvard freshman, Zuckerberg created Facemash to pit students against each other based on attractiveness. However, like Oprah Winfrey, Zuckerberg's initial attempt at leading in the digital space and building a great brand didn't work at his first attempt. Facemash was taken down.

Sticking to his aspirations to redefine social interactions, Zuckerberg and some of his friends created Facebook in their dorm room. It might not need voicing, but you might want to hear that Meta has over 1.5 billion daily users and is worth about $69 billion today (figures that most likely won't stop growing anytime soon).

The Loftiest Goal of a Personal Brand

Zuckerberg has clearly attained leadership status in the digital space (you only need to check out how many social media platforms have launched since then to believe this). But, beyond establishing his personal brand as a global leader in the social media space, he's also helped other individuals define or redefine their personal image and possibly become thought leaders.

That, my friend, is the peak of your achievements as a leader, influencer, and enviable brand. The summit of leading others is turning them into leaders themselves who also raise leaders. The cycle continues on and on in a spiraling chain toward transforming the world into a better place.

When applying the principles in this book toward stamping your image as a leader in a niche, you want to look toward influencing the next generation to replicate (or surpass) your feats.

That said, what is personal branding anyway? And why is it a vital leadership skill? Let's find out.

What Personal Branding Means

A personal brand is a story *you* tell about yourself. It's how you communicate your values and talent to your potential audience, colleagues, clients, and other professionals. People see it as what you do and stand for (whether or not it's true).

You want to realize that whether or not you tell your story, people already are. Both online and offline, every action or sublime action that gets in the public's eye defines your brand identity.

Personal Branding and Leadership Image

Why Does It Matter?

Everyone, teen, or adult, has a relatively short attention span than the world has ever seen. Similarly, making a solid impression that cuts through all the distractions and wrong voices is more important than ever.

The best way to achieve this is to create an unforgettable personal brand. Whether it's creating a successful business, advocating a social influence, or teaching a helpful skill, you won't do much without building a successful brand image.

Renowned American author and motivational speaker Zig Ziglar once summarized the benefit of building a great brand in this quote: 'If people like you, they will listen to you. But if they trust you, they'll do business with you.' Beyond making folks like you, having a solid brand image makes them *trust* you.

When you become deliberate about building a great brand, you control how you advertise yourself. You also can better manage your choices to build reliability and trustworthiness.

Even more: building a personal brand can help you become a more genuine version of yourself. That's because you have a firmer grasp of yourself and who you want to be. You're more likely to make choices and decisions that are more consistent with your values or goals, motivating you to become an even better leader and influencer for others. How better could it be?

The Four Cs of an Effective Personal Brand

This entire chapter addresses creating a personal brand to build a trustworthy leadership image. However, before we delve into the fundamentals of building an effective and enviable personal brand, let's see some vital elements of personal branding.

I call them the 4 Cs of effective personal branding. Everything you do toward building your dream brand should have these elements. They include credibility, content, character, and charisma.

1. Credibility

Understandably, social pressure has forced many young people into creating fake personal images of themselves online. You don't want to be part of it. Creating a fake brand will ultimately lead to one thing: inconsistencies.

Folks will, somehow, later catch up with the lies and lose all the credibility they built in you. Moreover, by being consistent with your values, principles, and voice, you can build trust in your brand and possibly gain more opportunities in your personal or professional life.

2. Content

As a teen, you definitely have various skills and talents or aspects to yourself. You possibly wouldn't project *everything* in a single brand. Here's where your brand's 'content' comes in.

Content is the value you offer. It's the sum of the skills, talents, and traits people connect with you. The contents you want to amplify will differ depending on the niche or industry you choose to lead,

You might also be a sportsman who wants to build a reputation for being an intelligent thought-leader on global issues. In contrast, another teen might want to project themselves as a trendy and hip fellow that others can follow for the latest commentaries on the latest fashion, music, or movie few people have heard of.

3. Character

Building a successful brand goes beyond fame or success. It also involves delineating and sticking to boundaries and principles you cherish. You want to position yourself as a person of integrity while preventing external forces from influencing you against your values.

Defining your stand can help you base your decisions on higher goals than money, such as personal satisfaction, fulfillment, commitment to ethics, and the happiness that comes from having no fear of being jinxed for being false or gravely inconsistent.

4. Charisma

You want to create a personal brand that stands you out from the competition. While it's clear no teen should be in unhealthy rivalry or competition, it doesn't change the reality that the world is full of too many people trying to make an impression – good or bad.

One quality that sets some apart from others and grants them more followers than others is charisma. What makes your brand story unique? Mind you, the answer to this question isn't as complex as it sounds. You only have experienced yourself, and you're more than competent to bring a rare blend of experiences to the table.

Next, we'll explore other critical aspects of creating a personal brand that projects the best leadership image you want – and how to apply them to your brand story.

You'll also learn various ways of adapting social media channels to boost your brand image while putting in place the right measurement metrics to judge your progress rate.

Utilizing Social Platforms to Enhance Leadership Influence

The pandemic era painted the world in a picture that beats anything this generation had seen. Lockdowns, social distancing, and the realities of remote work all forced a shift in how leaders in business, politics, religion, and even the entertainment industry influenced their followers or teams.

Social media is one tool that effectively saves the day more than many others. Beyond making the world a global village, social media is developing leaders by helping them grow their influence and network, offering them opportunities for relational and multilevel connections.

As promised, this section provides actionable tips you can apply to start growing your brand immediately. So, how do leaders leverage social media to influence their following?

How do you choose the best social media platform to air your unique brand voice? Find out answers to these questions and more in the next few paragraphs.

Steps to Harnessing the Power of social media in Enhancing Your Influence as a Teen Leader

1. What Do You Want to Achieve?

This partially relates to the second C in our 4 Cs of effective personal branding, but it's slightly different. Understanding what content you want to put out is important. But it's also important to have a clear vision and purpose for your goals as a leader.

Your content defines what value you intend to offer to your audience. What problems will your content solve in the world when people absorb them? How many people do you want to reach in the next six months?

Suppose your personal branding directly or indirectly involves converting value into money; your goals could also include monetary goals. How much do you intend to earn over the next year or couple of years? Remember, you want to set achievable goals from the outset to ensure you don't burn out or get under undue pressure because you missed targets.

Your purpose should center on why you want to lead. The brand's vision will guide your direction, while your mission shows you how to reach there. Understanding these points will ensure that all these points culminate in crafting an effective message that lets you reach your intended followership.

Your personal branding journey won't be a quick-fix regimen. You want to take enough time to do the work and gradually elevate your brand into a position of influential leadership.

2. Who Is Your Potential Audience?

Here's the place to define the prospective beneficiaries of your value. Clearly understanding the demography, behavioral patterns, and habits of your intended audience helps you better connect to them.

Who is your perfect audience, customers, clients, or followers? Do you intend to grow that circle with time? If you intend to grow your reach with time, that might affect how you build the basics or foundation for your brand. It could influence your brand's logo or brand name (to potentially reach a wider audience much later).

For instance, ladies and guys typically don't respond alike to information on sports, fashion, or food. The response gap is even wider between generations. A baby boomer will likely react differently to a comment on Irish Independence differently from teens, for instance.

In fact, one author once said, 'Age remains the best single data point when it comes to understanding what a voter thinks about politics.' Define your audience (or future audience) clearly and tailor your content with them in mind.

3. Choose the Right Social Media Platform and Format

Every social media platform performs just what it should do – connect people from different places and allow users to air their views. However, each social media platform has its unique features, strengths, and weaknesses.

You'd know too well that Instagram couldn't completely replace X (formerly Twitter) as we know them. And that you couldn't superimpose Reddit on WhatsApp. That gives a broad idea of what this step seeks to establish.

In the bid to leverage social media to position yourself as a thought leader in a niche or category, choosing the perfect platform to connect with your intended audience is invaluable.

Remember that your personal brand (or story) involves meeting a unique goal style and reaching a unique audience. You want to choose the right digital platform that fits hand-in-glove or *almost* does.

Suppose you intend to tell short and interesting stories. You might consider Instagram or X. Conversely, if you want to create videos that advocate a social cause or show your charisma, think YouTube, Facebook Live, Snapchat, or something similar. Similarly, long-form content will do well on LinkedIn or Medium.

Your audience type also determines the platform you select. While TikTok has many teens like you on it, LinkedIn has mainly business professionals, CEOs, and other members of the corporate industry. Audiomack has podcast lovers who probably love music or don't mind listening to longer-voiced recordings.

Here's also the place to consider the formats that best fit your content, such as texts, images, videos, podcasts, infographics, etc. Of course, you could consider blending these formats to entertain your viewership and possibly reach a wider audience.

4. **Create Valuable and Original Content**

Remember our first C of an effective personal brand? One key to building and maintaining credibility is to create valuable and original content for your audience. On the value side, you're offering your audience helpful information, solutions, or motivations. Originality means your content consistently reflects your voice, value, and flair.

A word of caution here: avoid being too salesy in projecting your leadership brand's value online. Rather, work toward being honest and authentic while being engaging. Teen leaders will do well to make their storytelling interesting through storytelling, humor, or appeal to emotions to lead the audience.

If you can, avoid contracting your contents for others to make them on your behalf. If you must outsource your content to a team, ensure your team understands your brand voice clearly enough to replicate your voice via your posts.

5. Engage

Social media requires two-way communication. You want to engage your audience to foster trust and grow connections. One way to engage them is to ask questions in your CTA, reply to comments, request feedback, or create quizzes.

You could also consider joining relevant groups or communities to expand your network and potential client base. If you have other teen leaders/influencers in your space or a related industry, consider collaborating with them to exchange ideas, create joint content, or jointly promote value.

6. Measure and Improve Your Performance

It's wasteful spending resources on a brand-building plan that doesn't pay. One way to avoid this is constantly or periodically measuring and monitoring your social media performance to see what strategy works and what doesn't.

Various tools for tracking your reach, conversions, and brand reputation exist. Analytics tools can also provide you with feedback to identify your weaknesses, opportunities, strengths, or threats (SWOT). After identifying the useful and the not-so-helpful, you're better prepared to adjust your content strategy or tactics toward improving efficiency and effectiveness.

Creating a Digital Footprint that Reflects Leadership Values

'Your digital footprint paints a portrait of who you are as an educator, leader, school, or district. Make sure it conveys your true values and work.'
– Eric Sheninger

While social media tells your story, your digital footprints go a step beyond to include what others say about you online. It provides a better representation of your image as a leader.

Regularly monitoring your reputation online will help you check for any negative or erroneous information as soon as it gets out. Understandably, it can prove challenging to care about what you put in the public's eye and what others broadcast about you.

Mention, Tweetdeck, and Hootsuite are a few tools to help you better monitor your personal image online.

With Mention, you can monitor any keywords related to you, your brand, your school, or any other relevant information to monitor. I fancy Mention because it goes beyond supervising on-the-web content (like blogs, news, and videos) to Insta stories, Facebook posts, and other social media content.

Tweetdeck and Hootsuite help to track your digital footprint on Twitter. You can easily track usernames, real names, hashtags, and city or school names with both tools.

Again, treat others kindly, avoid hurtful language, and exercise caution when addressing sensitive topics. While we're addressing conducting your brand's conversations right, remember that your digital footprint also extends to everything you say online.

Lastly, you want to ensure that all interactions, official or unofficial, don't contradict your declared goals or perspectives. So you don't want to sound helpful on Medium, for instance, while bullying others on your class's group chat.

You know too well that news spreads quickly when people want it *to* (especially negative stories)! It's a sad reality, but it's true, nevertheless.

In the final sections of this chapter on personal branding and leadership image, we'll address:

- The impact of appearance and style on leadership image
- Getting the right mentors and role models
- Networking effectively
- Mastering elevator pitches

The Impact of Appearance and Style on Leadership Image

You get into a room and find a leader who radiates an irresistible aura that makes heads turn and hearts skip. The atmosphere brims with excitement and belief in the leader. A bit of charm, a slice of magnetism, and a charismatic style is where the wonder begins.

There's no underestimating how valuable physical appearance could be in your image as a leader. Nathan shares his childhood story on Quora about being obese in his early childhood. He suffered both physically and emotionally as friends bullied him.

The result went beyond impairing his ability to make friends and enjoy childhood. It also got him depressed and introverted and forced him to cry himself to sleep every night.

At this point in his life, it's already clear that public opinion has impaired

Nathan's personal branding. His ability to influence his peers in school is highly limited, reducing his leadership potential.

Fortunately, Nathan took control of his life and achieved a healthy weight by 17. Even more, Nathan challenged himself to make adequate changes to improve his appearance with various physical fitness regimens to help him become a six-packed, well-groomed guy many young ladies (and guys) would love to associate with – just by his looks.

Young Nathan isn't alone. Many young people have bad prospects at leadership for a few other reasons than their looks. It might sound unfair; it's how we are wired.

According to a study by researchers from the University of Arts and Science in Oklahoma, having a 'babyface' was considered 'inconsistent' with qualities people want in a leader. The study also showed that people were more likely to follow other people they find attractive.

But the leadership image goes beyond physical appearance. It extends to your personality, speaking style, body language, and behavior. It determines whether your prospective audience eventually converts into actual clients or if they'll look away and hope for someone with your content but a *better* appearance.

Think Trump vs. Biden. It's no news that Americans voted for either candidate partially based on their 'personality,' body language, and public behavior.

Where necessary, pay attention to your outfit to project an image of someone people will be willing to heed. You want to authentically polish your physical appearance and style toward improving your leadership image and skill-up.

Remembering that your leadership image transcends physical appearance, work to excel in your personality and body language to situate yourself as a teen leader other young folks will want to associate with.

Mentorship and Role Models

You may have heard the term role model or mentor used interchangeably. Your classmate or friend, for instance, could have identified someone as their mentor or role model, and it might have got you thinking. Don't worry; you're not alone in the boat.

When I was younger, I had similar conflicts about defining role models or their *roles* around me. If there's any lesson I can confidently pass on to a beloved teen, it's to get their 'mentorship' game right.

By 'mentorship game,' I mean everything from getting adequate counsel and guidance for carving your path toward becoming an influential and impactful leader. It also means ensuring you get the right mentors who will be worthy oversights in guiding your leadership journey.

It's sad to admit, but even adults make mistakes, too (in many things, including mentoring and raising younger leaders).

Your goal is to become a mentor and role model to many teens and younger kids around you. You aim to reach beyond just your classroom or block to a wider audience online and offline. Awesome! But you're better prepared to quickly achieve your goals with the right mentors and role models.

As Sir Isaac Newton once said, 'If I have seen further, it is by standing on the shoulders of giants.' Of course, Newton didn't physically stand on the shoulders of bodybuilders in his day. He meant that others inspired some of his scientific ideas. We begin by differentiating between mentors and role models.

Delineating the Difference between Role Models and Mentors

My dictionary defines a role model as someone worthy of imitation. However, it doesn't conclude that the follower will imitate only excellent behavior. Someone could pick a role model with destructive behavior for whatever reason seemed best to them.

Apparently, the dictionary definition implies that a role model is someone a follower *feels* is worth copying. In contrast, a mentor often functions as a tutor who impacts mentees and pulls them up the leadership ladder.

Role models are typically the people you'd find in the news or on social media without direct access to them. Role models often can't help you closely monitor your choices or reprimand you for failing to achieve your aims. It's also easy to idealize or idolize role models since you know no other thing than their personal branding suggests.

Budding leaders find or assign mentors based on needs or as a result of direct two-way communications between mentor and mentee. Unlike role models, mentorship leaves all mystery behind and fosters a mutual relationship built on trust, openness, and a sense of responsibility.

Here's a handy table to help you better distinguish between a mentor and a role model

Mentor	Role Model
Professional	Public personality
Direct contact	No direct contact
No mystery	Idealistic
Built on mutual trust and openness	Doesn't need to build on mutual trust and openness
Good influence only	Potentially, good or bad influence
Conscious influence	Unconscious influence

Who Can Be Your Mentor or Role Model?

Who can be a role model to budding teen leaders? Virtually anyone, from athletes like Michael Jordan to businessmen like Elon Musk, politicians like Barack Obama or Trump, or Hollywood stars like Scarlett Johannson.

Beyond public figures, your role models could include family figures like your parents or religious figures like Rick Warren.

While you could take up role models from public figures who don't personally know you, you'll also need mentors with whom you can readily establish two-way communication. Basically, both roles are critical in your journey toward influencing the world around you.

Role models help younger people find their passion in a field of learning, a hobby, or a religion. They're often great inspirations to kick-start what could be a lifelong interest or culture.

However, mentors are (often) the people who convert the seed role models plant into reality. They're the tutors who hold your hand while you look toward the horizon and role models who inspired you to pursue. They range from teachers and counselors to parents and caregivers. Some mentorship platforms also let young people access direct mentorship from professionals in their chosen fields.

Why You Should Have a Role Model or Mentor

Choosing the ideal role model or mentor can be the singular difference between a budding teen leader who goes on to fulfill their dreams and another who fails along the line.

Once selected wisely, a role model can bring immense benefits and life-changing events. Suppose you're a teenage Nigerian immigrant seeking to excel in America's tech space.

Your arrival in the US comes with various cultural shocks and, maybe, internal fears. However, you're not aiming to become a top US engineer alone. You also would become wealthy enough to help fund social causes that matter to you.

One way to quickly set a North Star for yourself and start your journey toward national acclaim is by picking a role model in Nigerian-born Tope Awotona. The narrative says Tope poured his life savings into Calendly, a SaaS company, and worked his way to become one of the only two black billionaires in America.

And what if you aren't an immigrant, then you have Bill Gates, Jeff Bezos, or any other related natives as potential role models.

Another vital benefit of choosing a role model early enough is to give yourself a sense of purpose. A female athlete will likely feel overwhelmed in women's sports without a role model like Serena Williams or Riley Gaines, given the 2023 realities around the games.

On the other hand, mentors can help you develop your career by listening to your struggles and dreams. They're helping hands to help you better understand your talents and give you tools or even a platform to advance your goals.

Being professionals themselves, mentors can share their experiences with you, highlighting their challenges and mistakes to make your leadership journey less complex.

A role model won't be there to cheer you on when you did great or motivate you when you're struggling. But a mentor will. They'll be there to help you set the right goals and tasks, and often, they'll be there to cheer or rebuke you at the end of the journey.

Finding the Right Role Model

Finding the ideal role model might not be complex as they're almost always in your face. You only want to ensure you imitate a role model's good character that possibly made them become what you want to be.

On the other hand, one way to select or find the right mentors is effective networking. And we'll discuss effective networking in the next subsection.

Effective Networking

Networking is how we build and maintain relationships and contacts. People network to have a suitable group of contacts to draw on when they need help and support. From getting a new job to garnering important information or a listening ear in crises, your network can be helpful.

However, your network doesn't only include mentors and other tutors with whom you have 'two-way' communication. It also includes building horizontal relationships with other teen leaders and even mentees or (your) followers.

That's why the actionable networking tips I'll show you here relate to finding relevant mentors, partners, and even followers to enhance your leadership experience. So, what can you do as a budding leader to grow your network to include only people important to your life goals?

Be Deliberate about Building an Effective Network

Every teen has a network of people they relate with, but not everyone has an effective network. An effective network is a group of contacts on whom you can confidently hang your dreams.

You've got to be deliberate about what relationships you nurture and groom. Now, DON'T ignore folks because you think they won't benefit you. Instead, DO build a network that includes people you admire, enjoy spending time with, or think are crucial to your life, regardless of whether you like their company now or otherwise.

You won't need every individual in your circle all the time. Some are relevant only when you need help. Basically, create a network that could expand your network, not contract them.

Show Value for Existing Connections

'He who is faithful in little is also faithful in much,' goes a famous Biblical verse. And I absolutely agree with it.

Your best bet at building a network is showing value to existing relationships. Of course, one clear way to show value in a relationship is by investing your time into it. Whether it's sending a once-in-a-while message to connections to say, 'I just thought of you' or regularly reporting to mentors on your progress, showing value can go a long way.

Valuing your existing relationships prepares your character and mind for more delicate or valuable connections. Besides, you could appear more believable when you share with new or potential connections how much you value your current relationships.

How does telling a role model bump into that you've learned a lot about them through your mentor? It does a lot, including telling the role model you're a great and grateful learner. And who knows? That impression could convert the celebrity role model into a close-range mentor.

Leverage social media

Here's the place to apply ALL we learned earlier on harnessing the power of social media for effective leadership. For the record, if you're considering becoming a leader in a career or profession, LinkedIn is the place to be. X is another platform to get the attention of prospective connections via mentions, retweets, and comments.

Of course, other platforms can also bring you great connections. That's what social media was created for – building effective networks.

Lastly, maintain an up-to-date online process to avoid missing important messages, mentorship, or team-building opportunities. Your leadership as a teenager is as effective as your vertical and horizontal networks.

Leverage Networking Platforms

Various institutions and bodies create networking and mentorship platforms or events to foster vertical and horizontal connections. Your school, for instance, could have a mentorship platform to help students connect with the right mentors.

Then, you could find online networking platforms advertising mentorship or people meets. These are great places for meeting new folks.

Don't hesitate to follow up new contacts as soon as you're back from the event. Keep conversations going with them until you cement the relationship and hopefully get a return gesture.

So, you attend this networking event and meet students you think could make great additions to your team. How do you convince them to give you their contacts and believe in your brand?

The magical tool to achieve this is what is called the Elevator Pitch. The next subsection addresses mastering an elevator pitch to convince prospects to buy into your brand.

Elevator Pitch Mastery

Chris Westfall tells a story of how Elevator Pitches became a thing. Hollywood screenwriters used to plan to jump into unsuspecting executives on an elevator ride. These screenwriters would present their ideas in 30 seconds or until the ride ends.

There are other stories on the origin of elevator pitches, some attributing it to salespeople. But the plots really tow the same line. An elevator tool is a clear, engaging, and persuasive 30-45 second speech to sell your brand, product, or talent.

Today, it has become an essential networking tool for individuals, job seekers, entrepreneurs, and salespeople seeking career advancement.

Crafting an Elevator Pitch that Sells

Prepare a brief introduction to yourself and your brand. The elevator pitch should consist of only a few sentences, covering who you are and what you do. Think of a well-crafted Twitter bio or LinkedIn headline. Here are a few tips to craft a compelling elevator pitch.

- **Keep it Simple and Clear**

The best elevator pitches are clear, concise, and easy to understand. Shove all the complex vocabulary you learned during mentorship or schooling aside. Remember, your aim is to incite interest; you don't need to explain every detail about yourself or your brand.

- **Be Persuasive**

Why should someone choose you over other brands or leaders? The answer lies in your Unique Selling Proposition (USP). A USP sets you apart from the competition. It could be an expertise, a milestone achieved, or an award you received. Presenting your USP is vital toward winning your prospects over.

- **Use Storytelling Techniques**

Storytelling is a powerful technique to make your pitches less forgettable. Consider including an anecdote or story that shows what you do, why you do it, and why you need their partnership. You could tell a story about how you've helped a past client or the inspiration behind your idea.

- **Practice Delivery**

Practice your pitch delivery until it becomes almost instinctive. Video-record yourself, watch your body language while doing so, review your performance, and seek constructive feedback from others. The more comfortable you are with your pitch, the more confident you can deliver it.

- **Deliver Confidently**

Your practice sessions must have prepared you for a proper delivery. You want to project enthusiasm and confidence when delivering your elevator pitch. Ensure you're standing straight, making eye contact, and using positive body language.

Personal Branding and Leadership Image

- **Follow Up**

After delivering the pitch, you want to follow up with a 'Thank You' note or follow-up message. Doing so can help to keep prospects mindful of you and your idea.

2 Elevator Pitch Examples for Teens

Let's see three elevator pitch examples to give you a visual idea of a pitch and what to prepare toward an (un)expected meeting.

Example 1

When I thought of attending this event, I never imagined I'd be standing before a team of award-winning leaders in my field. My name is Jack Grealish, and I'm a sophomore at Texas State University and a Theatre Arts major.

I served as a movie director for the Faculty of Arts' annual movie night. Currently, I intern at the Vibes, where I invest my movie writing, directing, and producing skills to foster the organization's community advancement cause.

As a Personal Assistant to the Movie's Scriptwriter, I bring my experience in an on-the-ground awareness of the average college audience interdepartmental liaison in the organization. Thank you for listening. I'd appreciate it if you would consider me for any available roles.

Example 2

Here's another example from a Microbiologist.

I have a bachelor's in microbiology from Purdue. I've interned at MicroSeams, where I currently serve as an Assistant Laboratory Manager. My successes in that role include improving operating procedures, customer management, and record keeping.

I believe my strengths in laboratory management and food analysis could bring strategic development to the table as an employee in your organization. Thank you for your time. Can I have your email for subsequent checks with your team?

The two examples here involve speaking with a prospective mentor or boss. Whether you pitch to potential clients, mentors, or mentees, the idea of an elevator pitch is pretty much the same.

Check out my one-minute elevator pitch format in the workbook section toward enhancing your personal brand and leadership image.

Workbook 7

Hello, my name is ……………………. and I am completely a ……………….. degree or course in ……………….. at (School) with a minor in ……………….

1. I am interested in a career or a position or in working with you (on a) ………………. In the

    ………………. field (or industry).

I have been involved (during high school or college) in …………………..

And developed skills or talents in …………… I have also had an internship position (or employment or home-crafted experience) as a …………… with………… and found that I really enjoy …………………...

Do you mind working with me (or mentoring me, joining my team) or bringing me on your team as a ………….?

I'll be glad to know what you think about this. Thank you for your time.

Pay rapt attention to their response and ask relevant questions where necessary. Remember to exchange contacts, if possible, to keep the conversation with them ongoing.

Here are two exercises to help you hone your personal brand and image as a leader.

Create a 30-day social media plan to consistently provide value about your personal brand on selected social media channels.

Practice the elevator pitch you devised in the workbook section, deliver it to your friends, and ask for their constructive feedback.

Takeaway 7

The quality of your teen leader is as effective as your vertical and horizontal networks.

And while you seek quality relationships, remember this quote from Irish poet Oscar Wilde: 'Be Yourself. Everyone Else is Already Taken.'

Chapter 8

Leadership with Integrity and Social Impact

The glue that holds all relationships together – including the relationship between the leader and the led – is trust, and trust is based on leadership
– Brian Tracy

Building a Legacy for Positive Social Impact

Disabled people are typically marginalized in the job market. In the US, only 34% of disabled people are employed, according to the US News & World Report. A few years ago, a group of disabled colleagues posed a vital question. They wanted to know if Accenture could determine any relationship between inclusiveness (with respect to people with disabilities) and a company's financial performance.

Accenture took the challenge and sought to take an ethical lead by practicing 'ethical hiring', i.e., considering a larger percentage of marginalized populations for employment. According to a Forbes report, where this story was published, Accenture proved for the first time that ethical hiring was connected to improved financial performance.

Over a four-year period, the IT company registered 28% higher in revenue. Of course, you could expect the reaction of other companies after hearing of Accenture's feat. They were soon asking how to address disability inclusion in their workforce.

Leadership with Integrity and Social Impact

I admit this story doesn't exactly describe your realities as a budding teenage influencer (you don't likely own or lead a Fortune 5000 company already). But it clearly communicates the focus of this chapter: Leading with ethics, integrity, and social impact in mind pays much more than leading without these values.

We explore the tenets of ethical leadership and leading during a crisis while advocating your prized values with empathy and empowering others to follow in your footsteps. Remember, a successful leader doesn't just turn prospects into followers, but leaders who do the same to others. That's what I call the Ripple Effect of Transformational Leadership.

Let's get into the chapter already!

Ethical Leadership

Ethical leadership means leaders behave based on a set of values and principles most people recognize as a sound basis for the good of everyone. While some various principles and values fit into this definition, six fundamental elements of ethical leadership include leading with:

- Respect
- Responsibility
- Trust
- Fairness
- Honesty, and
- Transparency

Why Ethical Leadership is Important

Ethical leadership helps you inspire others to behave morally right. Setting the pace and pointing others toward ethical behavior increases your followers' chances of acting similarly.

Ultimately, ethical leadership could create a ripple effect that influences the entire community toward positive culture, heightened loyalty, and stronger emotional health.

To the leaders themselves, an ethical leader helps them build credibility and a positive reputation. When a leader fails to show respect or honesty, for instance, to those around them, they may heavily damage their personal brand and lose immense social capital.

However, you may have exhibited some unhealthy traits or habits before now. It's not over for your personal brand and leadership image. Continuing unethical behavior can further (or severely) damage your self-esteem and lead to unfavorable outcomes or failed chances to express your talents and gifts fully.

You don't want to be known as the guy or girl who snubs every other person or is biased toward a group of people. Your best bet right now is to imbibe the six basic elements of ethical leadership through the actionable steps I'll show you right now.

How to Enshrine Yourself as an Ethical Leader

Ethical leadership isn't as "lofty" and way above your comprehension as it sounds. It's more achievable than it might appear. Here are comprehensive ways to enshrine yourself as an ethical leader among your peers.

- **Define Your Core Values**

Besides the general rules of ethics, consider the morals your parents or guardians instilled in you. Were you raised to lend a helping hand to struggling folks? Did your elementary schoolteacher make you always say thank you after receiving a compliment or comment? Here's your chance to add some unique flavor to your brand.

Leadership with Integrity and Social Impact

Sadly, we live in a world where things that were wrong during your parents' days are now contemplated in the courts. The legal system changes over time and could revoke its ideas about what is right or wrong. But you don't want to base your core values on such a dynamic and unpredictable moral system.

Sit yourself down; ask yourself what matters most to you as an individual. Then align your brand with those priorities.

- **Create a Team with People of Similar Values**

Remember the need for a network that potentially improves your effectiveness as a leader? One way to identify those to bring into your inner circle is by fishing out those with identical values. Whether you're hiring volunteers, choosing partners, or finding mentors, having people who share your core values is critical.

Mind you: this doesn't mean you stereotype your inner circle with people with similar experiences or competences. That would make your network monotonous and less resourceful. On the contrary, you need people with varying experiences and skill sets in your inner network.

But a thin line must join you all together – shared core values.

- **Maintain Open Conversations**

Have you ever felt like your class president made decisions you considered selfish without even considering the class's opinion? That's similar to how your team members could feel unless you maintain open two-way conversations with them.

If more people were listened to today, we might have fewer calls for equity and social justice. Create a community where every member feels heard.

Of course, you possibly can't bend to the demands of every customer or partner. You want to create a forum for sharing feedback and provide follow-up explanations on why some actions are feasible and others aren't.

Consistently gathering feedback from your team helps you improve your leadership experience and propels your brand forward.

Having a sense of integrity as a leader is vital, as it boosts your followership's morale, respect, and trust.

- **Avoid Bias**

Every human has subconscious beliefs that are inherently erroneous. Call them biases or something else. But they're there, nonetheless.

Admitting your silent bias can be tough. But failure to practice self-awareness can lead to harmful consequences.

Identify your biases and wrong preconceived notions during sessions of self-examination. That way, you're better prepared to avoid unfairly treating any team member or clientele.

- **Admit Your Mistakes Openly**

Ethical leaders aren't scared of holding themselves accountable to their followership and owning up when they make things go south. Be honest, admit your errors, and apologize, if necessary, to pacify unhappy or disappointed followers or partners.

Admitting your mistakes openly and taking full responsibility for your negative actions presents you as a strong and caring leader. You'd come across as someone ready to stand by their team and see them through till they find solutions to problems, not a finger-pointer.

- **Practice CSR**

CSR is the short form for Corporate Social Responsibility. Brands practice CSR toward social accountability and a commitment to impact society positively.

It could involve promoting diversity and inclusion like Accenture did in our opening story, giving back to the community, or even treating your team with respect. Whatever CSR idea you implement. It'll likely leave your leadership image better than it was.

Adapting to Change

Sue English, a licensed family therapist in Naperville, says that many people hesitate to change because of the discomfort entering uncharted territories could bring. And you couldn't agree less.

A quick look at the unprecedented hardship that physical distancing brought to many communities shows just how hard adapting to change could be.

Think about the other time you had to relocate, leave the sports team, change your school, or suffer the loss of a friend. How did you cope with the following season? Did you quickly recover from past experiences and move into the new? Or did adapting cost you so much that you're yet to recover?

How quickly or successfully we adapt to changes can show our rating on a crucial trait of great leaders: **adaptability**.

The best leaders understand that change is inevitable. Even more, they're prepared for them and can steer the team through unexpected developments toward a safe haven.

On the other hand, when leaders don't adapt quickly to change, the team may start to feel stagnant or stuck, creativity and growth might stiffen, and you might reduce your chances of forming vital relationships.

A Word of Caution: Avoid Maladaptive Patterns

Instead of adapting to change, we might sometimes regress to maladaptive patterns that avoid the realities of the new.

A student who lost an internship opportunity could resort to denying they ever wanted the chance in a bid to cope with the loss. Meanwhile, the same student could have plainly admitted to the loss, nursed their hurts to heal, and prepared to perform better next time.

Besides denial, other harmful maladaptive patterns against change include repression, projection, and splitting. Instead of turning to maladaptive patterns, here are helpful tips to help you steer your team when the times are changing.

Tips to Adapt to Change

- **Accept the Change**

Accept that change is inevitable. By learning to accept this, you're better prepared to adapt when it occurs. Remember that the best opportunities present themselves when you're adaptable to change, and this event could mean more enormous opportunities are underway.

- **Keep a Positive Atmosphere**

Regardless of the ongoing changes, keeping a positive atmosphere is essential for success in your field. Having a mindset that welcomes potential changes with a positive attitude can help you better adjust when they come. One way to do this is to concentrate on the cloud's potential silver (or gold) lining.

So, suppose a law went through to stop students from using a social media platform to make content in school uniforms – an act that has formed a significant part of your brand's activities.

The effective leader was already mindful of such potential changes, will accept the law, and maintain a positive attitude toward their brand's overall goals. No backing down on the bottom lines in the face of changes.

- **Focus on Things You Can Control**

Upon discovering the unexpected (or expected) news that could change how you conduct your operations, your next important step is identifying things you can control – and focus on them.

What can you still achieve today to get things going in the right direction? It's time to pay attention to these things to keep morale and productivity high enough. Interestingly, a positive attitude and productive mind are also vital for chartering the new course for you and your team.

Here's also the time to take a break and reflect on your brand's goals. Identify any skills you can learn to develop your overall value and competitiveness. Realizing how much development you can bring to your career or brand can increase satisfaction, regardless of the current challenges of a new season.

- **Set New Goals and Work Toward Them**

Setting new goals can help you revitalize your mind, renew your objectives, and re-clarify your focus during changing life circumstances. Additionally, goals can help you better prioritize in the new season and divert your attention from worrying about the developments.

Doing this can help you remain positive as a leader and motivate your team toward sustaining or improving your productivity.

- **Stay in Touch with Your Team Members**

Your team members are likely also trying to cope with the new developments. One way to keep the atmosphere on your team upbeat is to maintain constant communication with them.

Ask them relevant questions, not just about their work, but even allowable questions about their personal (non-work) lives. Talking to them could even boost your spirits further as some might have brilliant ideas on navigating the new changes.

Staying in touch could just be what your followers need to maintain belief in your organization or brand. Don't ever leave your team during a crisis.

And that leads us to the next leadership lesson for building a legacy for positive social impact: Mastering Crisis Leadership.

Crisis Leadership

The story is told of a war general in medieval times who was asked during a war: 'How do you cope when there is no food for the soldiers but enemies to fight?' His reply? 'There's no problem, as long as the enemies have food.'

Talk about a leader who knows how to navigate a crisis aptly while meeting his team's goals.

A crisis is an event that interrupts your routine operations. Crises come in various severities, and worse scenarios could lead to reduced profits or impair a brand's reputation. It could be a pandemic, a natural disaster, a scandal (true or otherwise), or a brewing rebellion within your team.

Crisis leadership is the process of responding accurately to the challenges posed in a crisis and ensuring they don't reoccur in the future.

There's no situation where leadership is more critical than during a crisis. In fact, true leaders are known during crisis situations.

As Publilius Syrus famously said, 'Anyone can hold that helm when the sea is calm.' If you still don't get the drift, he meant it's easy to lead when things are going well.

Mastering crisis leadership won't only make you a pace-setting leader in your field; it can also place you in the best position to learn during hard times and bring new innovations to make the world more crisis-proof.

Crisis Management vs. Crisis Leadership

Unlike crisis management, which involves a reactionary strategy to restore normalcy after a crisis, crisis leaders also focus on the long-term implications of challenging developments.

As a teen leader, your goal isn't just to respond accurately to unwanted developments. You're creating a team ready to change methods or grounds in the face of opposition, difficulties, or a new era.

Before we round up this section, let's highlight the five components of effective crisis leadership.

- **Recognize Early**

Some crises can grow gradually, making it difficult to recognize them early enough before they severely impact your team. Whether or not a negative develops slowly, its impacts might not become apparent until much later.

Effective leaders recognize problems early and work quickly with crisis managers to reduce their effects on the team. Research possible events that could negatively affect your brand. Then create an emergency response plan or mindset to address the situation.

- **Remain Optimistic**

Remember when I explained maintaining a positive atmosphere during an unwanted change? Remaining optimistic doesn't mean you undermine a crisis' severity.

However, it lets you accurately comfort your employees and clients while staying sensitive to the impact of the development on their lives.

Suppose you were communicating with your team after you lost in a major competition. A crisis leader will express their regret for lost resources in the build-up to the event while announcing they're confident about the team's ability to recover and win more contests in the future.

- **Reestablish Your Priorities**

When making decisions, a crisis leader revokes the team's priorities or core values.

An ethical crisis leader might prioritize the (emotional, physical, and psychological) well-being of their clients and team members.

These leaders prioritize human lives over other needs. An example is closing your team's activities when there's a hurricane in the city to ensure physical health. The crisis leader also wants to recall the organization's secondary priorities.

So, during a hurricane, for instance, you could create a system of communicating regularly with your team (e.g., weekly) to keep them in the loop. Communication becomes a secondary value compared to physical well-being in such cases.

- **Request for Additional Support**

It's common to find leaders struggling to retain power during a crisis. However, there's nothing wrong with requesting additional support.

Consider contacting mentors for counsel on managing the development. Also, delegate crisis management roles to other stakeholders. Acknowledging various schools of thought and ideas shows you respect others and gives your team members a sense of purpose during difficult times.

- **Revise Your Strategy**

Revising your strategy suggests adaptability. Good crisis leaders can easily revise their plans as the event progresses. The first emergency plan you set up to manage a crisis might not suffice after a few days or weeks.

Suppose communicating weekly with the team during a hurricane doesn't help you sustain your followers' interest. Consider organizing online meets to foster an increased sense of belonging and participation.

- **Advocacy and Activism**

The US Constitution gives all citizens (including young folks) the right to advocate for a change in the US. Meanwhile, the First Amendment to the American Constitution protects the rights of groups and individuals, advocating changes in government practices, laws, and even the form of government.

But these are just two expressions of many rights every American has.

Sadly, in the wake of the crisis, governing institutions tend to marginalize the rights of vulnerable segments of society, including racial minorities, immigrants, and younger people.

Good leaders stand up to defend the rights of others and pursue those rights via constructive activism.

Even more, good leaders don't just stand up to wrong practices in governance or vices among the citizenry. They're great at mobilizing others in their community to leverage the power of unity in enforcing the change they want to see in the world.

Mind you: you don't have to start with the intention of changing a law your governor passed. You could begin by advocating for more orderliness among students using public facilities in your school.

Advocates and activists dedicate some of their resources to positively impacting the world. How about we see some teen advocates who have led the charge on social change globally?

Greta Thunberg

When Greta was 15 in 2018, she protested outside the Swedish parliament's limits against climate change. She started a school strike for the climate, mobilizing other students to skip school to help save the planet.

Her calls for the country's government to pressure political leaders to meet carbon emission targets attracted worldwide attention. She inspired thousands of other young persons from various countries, including the US and Japan, to organize similar strikes.

Greta was named TIME Magazine's 2019 Person of the Year for her climate change activism. She has been considered a top contender to win the Nobel Peace Prize for her climate activism every year since 2019.

Malala Yousafzai

Malala Yousafzai attained a symbol of international repute for the fight for girls' education after surviving a gunshot while in a school bus by members of the Taliban. The Taliban maintains a school of thought that holds restrictions against female education.

Malala survived, recovered, and converted her experience into motivation for pursuing her fight. (Note the crisis leadership in Malala here!)

By 17, she had established the Malala Fund, an organization dedicated to giving girls a chance to learn and lead. She also became the youngest Nobel Prize laureate for her humanitarian efforts. Malala later published her book titled *I Am Malala* and graduated from Oxford in 2020.

Param Jaggi

When Param Jaggi was 16, he invented the Algae Mobile, a device that can convert carbon dioxide emissions from automobiles into oxygen. His contributions to creating clean and sustainable energy included him in the Forbes 30 Under 30 list.

Xiuhtezcatl Martinez

Xiuhtezcatl (pronounced shoe-TEZ-chat) is a 19-year-old indigenous climate activist, musician, and influential voice in the global youth-led climate justice revolution.

Martinez was inspired by his mother's activism from a young age and started joining the environmental movement at age 6.

He serves as the youth director of Earth Guardians, a nonprofit that trains various youths toward becoming leaders in the environmental and social justice space via leveraging art, music, storytelling, and legal action.

Abigail Lupi

Abigail became aware of the struggles nursing home residents face after visiting her grandmother in a nursing home at age 10. She created the CareGirlz organization to comfort and support these residents.

She helps nursing home residents by matching young volunteers with patients, making them feel loved and less lonely.

Greta Thunberg. Malala Yousafzai. Xihuhtezcatl Martinez. Abigail Lupi. Param Jaggi. If you never heard about these global teen leaders before now, you have.

All these leaders, and many others like them, have lent their voices, mobilized young people like them, or even influenced older ones to see the world through their eyes.

Meanwhile, did you see the various ethical leadership qualities in these figures? I bet you did.

Empowering Others

Like any of the five leaders we highlighted earlier, good leaders empower others to become better at being themselves. Better still, they inspire others to carve their voice and lead others into pushing unique causes or brands.

The dictionary defines empowerment as giving authority or power to someone so they can do something.

Good leaders fight for others. Great leaders empower others to fight for themselves. That's because one of the best ways to combat oppression, discrimination, and marginalization is through education and empowerment.

By educating others about the various forms of oppression and marginalization, how they could manifest, and their potential impacts on individuals and communities, you can equip them to challenge and dismantle oppressive systems.

Advocacy and activism, expressed in rallying people to protest and rally against wrong causes, can give people a voice to challenge injustice.

However, mobilizing people who understand little about the dynamics of the cause they're promoting can be counterproductive. Teens who take the pain to teach and empower others are more motivated to learn about their passion.

As an African proverb alludes, you don't want to be a one-eyed king in a community of blind folks.

Next, I sum up some of the vital ethical leadership qualities we've learned and show you how they spiral into the Ripple Effect.

The Ripple Effect: The Transformative Power of Empathy in Leadership

Sarah is a teen leader in her final college year. She has mastered the art of embodying empathetic leadership. She appreciates each team member's concerns, aspirations, and experiences.

She extends her empathetic approach beyond team morale into developing a common sense of commitment and purpose to team success. Under her leadership, her team of five other teens has metamorphosed into one of the most high-performing teams among comparable groups.

Leadership with Integrity and Social Impact

Her team constantly beats its goals and inspires others with excellence and comradeship.

In contrast, Susan is also a teen leader in her penultimate year at college. To her, empathy is a foreign concept exclusive to NGOs or government authorities.

Her focus, instead, is solely on meeting performance metrics and assignments. You'd often find her overlooking her team members' individual needs and experiences.

The result? Susan's team spirals downward, cutting from six initial members to three unconvinced hopefuls. She's surprised about why her team lost her best talents, who showed immense passion for their cause.

Her unwillingness to be empathetic continues to be a source of pain for her current members, who keep wasting resources in achieving a dragging cause. She's frustrated that her dedication to hard work has produced little result despite the rigorous academic activities.

Susan might be confused about the cause of her dilemma, but you need to watch Sarah's leadership style to understand the underlying cause.

Sarah's empathetic leadership style doesn't just nourish those around her; it has facilitated a nurturing climate where her team members have budded their growing teams. That is, in effect, the ripple effect in action.

The Ripple Effect in Action

Relationships risk becoming transactional and losing genuine connection when empathy is not in place. Without sympathy, misunderstandings escalate, many more people feel unheard or unappreciated, and communications break down.

Like you, young people need a place to express themselves. When you don't show empathy in their dealings with their followers, they breed an environment of dissatisfaction, disengagement, and attrition as people fight to seek fulfillment elsewhere.

Conversely, when you embrace empathy, you're likely to nurture trust, enhance collaboration, and boost effective communication. That helps you create a foundation for vibrant and lasting relationships.

Remember, you rarely can tell if, when, or how much you'll need some connections around you. However, showing empathy in various subtle and overt ways can put you in a special place in their hearts, cementing the possibility of receiving lasting goodwill from them.

Resilient Leadership

Every leader experiences stress and adverse situations. One thing, however, that sets high-performing leaders apart is resilience.

Resilience is the human capacity to meet setbacks, trauma, and adversity and recover from them toward normalcy and possibly improved experiences. Resilient teen leaders can sustain their energy level under pressure, cope with crises, and steer their teams to adapt successfully.

Resilient leaders don't just bounce back from setbacks; they overcome significant challenges without harming others or engaging in ethical behavior.

In addition to mastering ethics, value creation, and personal branding, BE RESILIENT.

Resilience is why Abraham Lincoln waded through eight election losses, two business failures, and a nervous breakdown on his journey to the White House. It's why Thomas Edison stayed on his light-bulb experiment 999 times before hitting the Eureka moment. It's why Nelson Mandela held to the hopes of ending apartheid through 27 years of imprisonment before becoming South Africa's first black leader.

Leadership with Integrity and Social Impact

During his imprisonment, Mandela mastered self-leadership, gleaning inspiration from a quote from the poem Invictus. The famous poem ends with the verse, 'I am the master of my fate/I am the captain of my soul.' True to those words, Mandela successfully led South Africans to become the captains of their land.

The Four Aspects of Resilient Leadership

You and your team have various life areas that directly or indirectly affect your performance. Showing resilience as a leader cuts across these four areas. Here are the four core aspects of resilient leadership.

Physical Resilience

A physically resilient leader has the body capacity to respond to stressors with stamina and strength. They can quickly recover from injury, stress, or discomfort and get going.

Otherwise, they can manage their strengths during moments of ill health without letting important tasks suffer grievously.

Emotional Resilience

Emotional resilience refers to understanding, appreciating, and regulating your feelings as a leader. The emotionally resilient leader deliberately chooses among feelings and responses.

They aren't unhealthily spontaneous, automatically reacting to events in their environment.

Mental Resilience

Mental resilience is retaining your cognitive abilities in the face of stress or other threats while allowing creativity to emerge. A mentally resilient leader can stay productive even under stress or pressure.

They're also better able to recover an atmosphere that allows constructive reasoning if a crisis or unwanted situation unsettles them.

The good news about these four aspects of resilience is that you can improve in every aspect and inspire others to do the same.

Becoming a More Resilient Leader

Remember, even if you aren't leading a team now as a teenager, you're already leading yourself. That's why you want to start applying the leadership tips in this book to your long and short-term goals.

By consistently leading yourself rightly, you're transforming yourself into a story others would love to learn from or follow.

That said, how can you become more resilient as a leader?

- **Boost Mindfulness**

It doesn't matter whether you're celebrating a milestone or going through a notably tough time. Set time aside for mindfulness. Mindfulness creates an environment that fosters self-awareness, learning, and novel ideas that can enhance mental resilience and facilitate resilient leadership.

- **Increase Physical Activity**

Physical activity lowers your blood pressure and cholesterol levels. Additionally, regular exercises improve your ability to process and quickly respond to stress. That way, you can have less time on the hospital bed, improve your physical resilience, and make your leadership more impactful.

- **Get Adequate Sleep**

Intelligent workers know how to work efficiently – including learning when to rest. Scientific research has proven that taking a break from work and making time for at least seven hours of sleep can strengthen your chances of being a resilient leader.

Adequate sleep goes beyond nurturing your body to improving your mental alertness, making you better equipped to manage unexpected developments while being empathic.

Leadership with Integrity and Social Impact

- **Confront the Status Quo**

The status quo refers to an accepted way of doing or knowing things, what they mean, how they work, or why things happen. It's the rote. If there's one thing to take from becoming emotionally and mentally resilient, it's this: Never take the status quo as-is.

Many scientific improvements over the centuries have deliberately or unintentionally broken the status quo and glass ceilings. Some schools of thought older people hold or pass down are potentially faulty, especially when they don't cross the boundaries of ethics and morality.

Learn to spot these potentially faulty assumptions about what others think or how they do things. Alongside your team or like-minded friends, conduct a cognitive reappraisal to challenge the potential fault lines of these assumptions.

When facing a crisis, challenge the assumptions the events throw at you. When your body is well rested, and you're less stressed, consult with your team to analyze the prospects of the crisis to arrive at more productive beliefs.

- **Practice Gratitude**

No matter your current level of resilience, grit, or following, gratitude will make you a better leader. Take time to acknowledge and appreciate team members who contributed to your cause throughout the day.

Meanwhile, the more deliberate you are about being thankful to your team, the more chances you have of triggering a feeling of gratitude in your team.

- **Build Social Connections**

You couldn't overemphasize the need to build valuable social connections toward becoming a transformational leader.

Build social connections by developing and nurturing a broad personal and professional relationships network. You want to build vibrant relationships with mentors, family members, team members, and other leaders.

Building social connections and sustaining them requires a level of emotional and mental well-being. Sustaining these connections will help you grow your resilience as a leader and become better at driving toward your brand's goals.

- **Engage Your Senses**

Engaging your senses can help reduce anxiety and stress.

It ranges from taking some time off sightseeing or vacation off-work to playing a car racer console game to reduce stress and anxiety.

What senses do you use to improve your resilience as a leader?

Everyone. All, including your sense of touch.

Scientific research has proven that physical contact can reduce stress and improve activity. Even brief touches, like a high-five or fist bump, can enhance your overall well-being.

In remote/hybrid work environments, touching others can be misunderstood or considered inappropriate. If you're in a similar team or situation, you can better practice resilience in your personal life, sharing contact with helpful people – and your pets.

Transformative Leadership

You don't have to spend too many years in the world to know that there are different kinds of leaders.

The unethical ones. The rash. The mean. The influential. The activist. Interestingly, many leaders who turn out bad never wanted to be so when they were younger.

Do you know what affected their leadership success? Their failure to adhere to some, most, or all of the principles highlighted in this manual.

A good leader is ethical, empathetic, and resilient. They empower their followers, advocate for social justice, and can adapt to changes. If I were to sum up all these qualities in one term, you have what I call the Transformative Leader.

What Is a Transformative Leader?

The Transformative leader can inspire changes in their followers. They're generally energetic, passionate, and zealous, are seen as such, and can readily pass these qualities to their team members.

They can readily take control of a situation by communicating a clear vision of their team's goals.

The concept of transformational leadership was first introduced by MacGregor Burns, a historian and leadership expert who tells the life stories of America's presidents.

Burns defined transformational (or transformative) leadership as a situation where leaders and followers help each other advance toward higher motivation and morality.

In contemporary times, Bernard Bass, an American psychologist, built on Burns' ideas to create the Bass' Transformational Leadership Theory.

You need to know that Bass' theory has become widely accepted among leadership experts and faculties worldwide.

You want to know what this leadership expert thinks about how you can be a great leader.

Bass' 4 Components of Transformational Leadership

Bass says there are four components of transformational leadership:

- Intellectual stimulation
- Individualized consideration
- Idealized influence
- Inspirational motivation

According to Bass, transformative leaders encourage creativity in their followers. They encourage their team to explore new ways of doing things, challenge the status quo, and seek new learning opportunities.

Moreover, transformational leadership also involves encouraging and supporting each follower. The transformative leader is supportive, keeping clear communication lines open so their followers can share their ideas.

Beyond being considerate and intellectually stimulating, transformative leaders act as their followers' role models. They can influence their team to trust and respect the leader, which makes them emulate their ideals, values, or goals.

Lastly, transformational leaders can clearly articulate their vision to their followers. They do this well enough to help them experience the same motivation and passion they experience toward achieving shared bottom lines.

The last quality of a great leader that positively impacts their team for social change is sustainable leadership.

After addressing sustainable leadership, you'll learn about a topic most leaders (and maybe you) want to know about – balancing leadership with the leader's personal life.

So, what does sustainable leadership look like?

Sustainable Leadership

Sustainable leadership is a management approach that highly considers what world leaders call the SDG Goals – Sustainable Development Goals.

You've probably heard about it. If you haven't, the United Nations' SDG Goals include 17 target actions to transform our world.

They include a call to action to end poverty and inequality, protect the planet, and ensure everyone enjoys health, justice, and prosperity.

Now, you don't want to be a leader who neglects the loftiest developmental goals of the United Nations, especially in a highly globalized world.

In your little ways as a budding teen leader, your best goals should factor into solutions that solve environmental, social, and economic problems around you.

That, in summary, is sustainable leadership.

A sustainable leader understands that the world is growing complex daily and embraces that fact. There are consequently more long-term thinkers who are adaptable to change.

Why Sustainable Leadership is Important

Remember Param's drive to create tools to convert carbon dioxide from automobiles into oxygen? Malala's drive to foster girl-child education? Or Martinez, who's driving the revolution for climate action despite being a hip-hop star?

Each of these leaders is, in effect, sustainable in their approach to influencing others.

Like Xiuhtezcatl Martinez, you could lead your followership in multiple areas, selling your gifts and talents to the world while inspiring them through your advocacy for social change.

How about taking some time off your public speaking engagement to remind your audience about the need to dispose of waste appropriately?

How you combine your brand's activities into a transformative and sustainable leadership brand is left to you.

But you don't want to neglect these important factors while building your leadership career.

Balancing Leadership and Personal Life

As I said, one of the most frequently asked questions from growing leaders worldwide is this: How do I balance my leadership responsibilities with my personal life?

Leading ten, a hundred, or a million young people is something many young people look forward to. However, the challenges and responsibilities of leadership could be so choking that leaders have little time for their personal lives.

We recommend various ways to arrive at the leadership-personal life balance.

Meanwhile, let's see the signs that you might be suffering from a leadership-personal life imbalance and why you should balance your public and personal life.

Signs You Have an Unbalanced Leadership-Life Dynamic

- You spend so much money outsourcing your tasks, such as the laundry, meals, and dishes, waiting till you may have the time to do them yourself.

- You get easily irritated with your co-workers.

- You notice you're increasingly distancing yourselves from your loved ones (even when there isn't any logical reason outside work for such distance).
- Everything feels boring or unimportant when you aren't at work.
- You can't imagine doing what you do for the rest of your life. Even if you lead a cause you're passionate about, you don't think you should drive the cause *the way* you're doing so for the rest of your life.

Benefits of Attaining the Leadership-Personal Life Balance

Properly balancing life and leadership means you can avoid burnout during crisis periods.

It increases your chances of thinking creatively and achieving a higher success level.

Meanwhile, leaders' physical and mental health is threatened when they don't balance between their public and private lives.

According to a study, people who work more than 55 hours have a higher risk of having stroke, anxiety, and depression. Another study proves that working longer hours can lead to a physical decline in people's health.

You don't want to be a transformational or sustainable leader with poor health or an unsustainable relationship with family and friends.

So, how do you balance leadership responsibilities and the demands of your personal life?

1. Plan All Activities Ahead of Time

Decide from the start that you intend to combine work with leisure, fitness, or social activities. If, for instance, you find yourself in various virtual meetings with little breaks in-between and a remote workspace, you may want to call a friend over to work with you or take a call outside.

2. Schedule Your Tasks

Designate time for various tasks, including checking/responding to messages, taking meetings, or doing mentally intensive work. Scheduling tasks also helps you anchor them around your most-productive times.

3. Have a Work Closing Time

You'll almost always have work to do if you have time. Include in your tasks schedule a closing time to end the day's work.

To succeed at this, consider using technologies or gadgets that power down your work devices, lock your workspace once it's time to close, or at least remind you that it's time to rest for the day.

4. Enjoy Lunch with Friends and Family

Even if you're leading from your home, consider taking time out for lunch with friends or family. The change in environment promises to refresh your mind from the routine of work/leadership. Plus, you'll also have enough time to eat and get your body refreshed too.

5. Practice Self-Awareness

Self-awareness (also called mindfulness) makes it difficult to ignore imbalance.

Helpful techniques to maintain or improve self-awareness include meditation or breathing awareness. You could also take some time to reflect on your leadership/life balance goals toward reviewing your balance level so far.

By paying attention to your feelings, you might easily notice you're possibly restraining an important need to work. For instance, getting back to work can be challenging if you hear your stomach rumbling or remember you haven't fulfilled your promise to a beloved.

Workbook 8

- ✓ What are the core aspects of leadership resilience?
- ✓ Outline each aspect and examine your current resilience level in each part.
- ✓ Speak with your trusted friends or family about what they think about your self-evaluation of your resilience.
- ✓ Re-align the opinions of other TRUSTED friends or families with your opinion of your resilience as a leader.
- ✓ Identify areas to improve and become more resilient.
- ✓ Create a plan to improve your resilience and become a better leader and social advocate others would love to emulate.
- ✓ Execute your resilience-building plan for one month.
- ✓ Re-check with your TRUSTED folks or partners about what they think about your new resilience level.

Here's one exercise to keep the lessons learned in this section:

Look out for older or more experienced ethical youth (or teen) leaders in your niche or desired field. Outline their practice of ethical leadership you may want to imbibe into your leadership experience. Finally, send them a request to partner with them or get their mentorship.

Takeaway 8

Good leaders fight for others. Great leaders empower others to fight for themselves.

Never take the status quo as-is.

Many leaders who turn out bad never wanted to be so when they were younger!

Chapter 9

Leadership in a Changing World

I believe you learned a lot already about improving your value as a leader in your world.

However, this book – and your leadership experience – will be incomplete unless you imbibe some of the qualities I'll explain here.

The Digital Era

Humanity has seen three major eras in its economic history: the age of agriculture, the age of industry, and now, the digital age.

Agricultural practices became outdated during the industrial age. And so are industrial management practices unhealthy for the digital era.

If you're a teen leader reading this, you were born after 2002. It means you were born right into this world when things were about to go 'digital.'

As a photo alt-text from a Forbes article puts it, the production of iPhones signaled the beginning of the digital era.

In the last chapter of this book, you'll understand leadership in the digital age and how it helps you adapt to a globalized planet. The book closes with tips on maintaining a healthy relationship with technology.

However, I won't let you finish this chapter without also showing you how to administer:

- Activism and leadership for social Change
- Mental health and well-being in leadership
- Ethical leadership in the business world
- Strategies for navigating ambiguity and ambivalence
- Building a Legacy
- Leaving a positive impact and inspiring future generations
- Maintaining a healthy relationship with technology

Let's learn the tricks and tips for an outstanding, responsible, and influential teen leader in the digital age.

Leadership in the Digital Age

In a world where bytes have accrued more value than atoms, you couldn't possibly overemphasize the need for a new kind of leadership that leverages technology to drive sustainable development globally.

Meanwhile, you might better appreciate leadership in this age by contrasting it with how top executives led industries and production lines decades ago.

For instance, the industrial age suffered from a steep vertical hierarchy of authority. Leaders told and coerced their team members what to do – and possibly punished, queried, or fired them for not following orders.

Conversely, the digital age requires a horizontal network of talents composed of self-managing teams pursuing a single goal.

While the industrial age focused mainly on how its internal activities can lead to outputs, the digital age leader concentrates on providing value for end users.

Finally, the digital age leader wants to engage the hearts of his followers, inspiring them toward collaboration and creativity rather than engaging their brains to increase production.

What Does Successful Leadership in the Digital Era Feel Like?

Successful leaders of digital firms have benefited the world in every aspect of human living. They've changed how people play, work, shop, learn, entertain themselves, read books, watch movies, or travel.

Successful leaders of digital firms have become immensely rich. Think Amazon, Apple, Facebook, Microsoft, or Calendly. Meanwhile, industrial-age firms like General Electric and IBM have struggled despite making heavy investments in Information Technology.

Of course, this isn't assuring you of stupendous wealth when you apply digital-era leadership skills to your NGO. However, it shows you the immense potential to boost your brand's value and worth by applying the digital era thinking to your leadership activities.

Developing the Digital-Age Leader

The Learning and Performance Institute, a UK-based independent global body for learning professionals, defined leadership development in the digital age as: 'equipping leaders with the digital skills and knowledge they need to lead their teams effectively in a digital world.'

Understanding how subjects like data analytics, AI, and process automation work will go a long way in positioning you for excellent leadership.

However, leadership in the digital age goes beyond understanding how technology works. Let's see other important traits of a digital age leader that are rarer in the industrial or agricultural eras.

Beyond Digital Age Literacy

Beyond digital literacy, a successful digital-age leader also needs to show other attributes like:

- Creativity
- Communication
- Empathy
- Collaboration
- Critical thinking
- Emotional Intelligence
- Agility/Adaptability

Empathy helps a leader support innovation and creativity from team members.

A report from Catalyst, an American not-for-profit organization, showed that institutions with empathetic leaders had a higher innovation rate than those without compassionate heads.

Meanwhile, when your team members feel valued, they'll more likely contribute to developing new solutions, services, and products.

Being empathetic, showing high levels of emotional intelligence, and imbibing digital-age skills can make you a better fit to lead an increasingly globalized world.

Adapting to Globalization

Whether you want to be a leader of global influence or otherwise, you already *potentially* are.

Every post you place on social media. Every word you say in public (or even in your dorm or closet). Everything you do today has the potential of going viral or public for everyone to see.

You know this too well.

With CCTV cameras, already globalized social media platforms, and other intelligence networks you don't know exist, every teen leader can't possibly avoid adapting to globalization in the digital era.

Use intolerant language on your class's Facebook group, and you risk losing the confidence of your growing followership.

Adapting to globalization means you're not only conscious of a highly connected world. It also means you're building your personal or corporate brand to accommodate globalization.

Three Simple Ways to Adapt to Globalization

Charles Darwin argued that the most surviving organisms aren't the most intelligent or powerful but the most adaptable. His assertion holds in today's fast-changing world.

The modern team (or team leader) must be adaptable, tolerant, and close to their customers or end users while also staying prepared for the future.

- **Open-Mindedness**

Open-mindedness is crucial to staying relevant in a world where the latest iPhones don't last more than a year before they become replaced.

Now, this isn't saying you have to buy the latest gadgets or purchase the most expensive subscriptions to adapt to globalization.

Instead, in part, it means you're flexible enough in your decision-making processes to accommodate new ideas, tech tools, and people.

- **Cultural Inclusiveness**

Talking about adapting to people. Ensuring your team adapts to people from various backgrounds helps you stay culturally inclusive.

Create cultural awareness and respect for other cultures. That, among other things, creates joint ownership and accountability.

Being culturally tolerant increases your team's (or followership) chances of including people from more cultures and backgrounds. That, of course, gives you higher hopes of receiving better ideas to drive your brand's goals.

- **Responsiveness**

Responsiveness means you're adaptable to new changes in the world around you as a leader.

But beyond this, you're sensitive to the needs or concerns of your employees. It means you're sensitive to local needs while ensuring your brand has a global appeal.

It also means being responsive to your clients, followers, or end-users. Create a feedback system that regularly checks on what others think about your brand and what they think about your services.

This subsection in one sentence?

Quickly get your brand on the globalization train before you get left behind for lack of versatility, intolerance, or agility.

Environmental Leadership

There's no discussing SDGs or the modern world without alluding to green technology.

Humans live on the earth today because it is commodious for us.

While I wish Elon Musk good luck with his plans to make Mars somewhat habitable, you and I have no other option than to work to create greener processes that protect human, animal, and plant existence.

However, as Binfeng Xu, a researcher from the University of Science and Technology of China, and his team suggest, followers will better show green innovation behavior under an environmental leader.

You might not dedicate all your time to advocating social change like Greta Thunberg or creating a product that turns carbon dioxide to oxygen like Param Jaggi.

But you can stay environmentally conscious enough to influence your followers toward upholding the principles of green innovation and technology.

How Anyone Can Imbibe Environmental Leadership

1. Understand the World's Environmental Issues

Understand the current environmental issues plaguing the world around you. You also want to discover what challenges and opportunities are available within your market to create innovative and creative solutions that appeal to green technology.

2. Make It a Priority on Your Team

For your team to become environmentally conscious, you must be the chief advocate for the environment.

You want to make environmental sustainability part of your organization's values and culture.

By emphasizing SDG goals, such as proper resource management for equity, a healthy lifestyle, and overall well-being, during meetings, you're preparing your team toward being more environmentally conscious.

3. Develop Metrics for Change

You can only introduce changes into metrics you can measure. After creating your blueprint for an environmentally conscious team, you want to develop measurable metrics to track your team's progress.

Measure everything from how much paper you use to data consumption and how often your in-house team members or leaders report ill health due to overwhelming work. Consider regularly presenting the metrics during meetings to encourage or motivate others to make more changes.

4. Promote It

One way to promote environmental leadership is via corporate social responsibility activities. You can do this either via social media messages or little offline projects.

The more people understand how committed your team is to promoting sustainability, the higher their chances of buying into your company's offerings or staying loyal to your brand.

Activism and Leadership for Social Change

The inspirational teen leader is a change agent who works to educate, organize, and involve others to actively stand for/against existing policies toward constructive solutions.

That, in effect, is what Bill Moyer, a leading American journalist, thinks you should be as a social activist-leader. And I agree with him.

Like Bill Moyer recommends in his handout on the Four Roles of Social Activism, a socially responsible leader isn't just a change agent.

They understand and accept their status as responsible Citizens, Reformers, and Rebels against unhealthy policies.

What does being effective in each of Bill Moyer's roles mean for you as you work toward building your resume as a social activist-leader in an increasingly globalized world?

The Effective Citizen-Leader

Here, you acknowledge that you're also a citizen of a nation and not just a leader 'in the middle of nowhere.'

At your best, you'd promote positive national values, symbols, and principles. You'd also encourage others to *show* their disinterest in a negative public policy for the common good.

Think Mandela or Martin Luther King.

The Effective Reformer-Leader

At their best, the effective reformer-leader leverages mainstream systems and institutions like the legislature, the assembly hall, or the school's official end-of-year meet to push their causes.

They'd also closely monitor the success of their promoted values or changes while protecting their cause against backlash.

The Effective Rebel-Leader

Of course, you're sure I won't write about rebelling against established authorities or the American Dream and sell it to you in a book. At least not overtly.

The effective rebel-leader protests against violations of positive, widely held values. Their approach is nonviolent, and their targets rally around government houses and CEOs' offices.

They present themselves tactically and strategically without being anti-authoritarian.

The Effective Change Agent/Leader

As an effective change agent/leader, you influence your team to promote a paradigm shift via strategies and tactics that promote long-term social advocacy.

You're also ready to educate others on the cause you're promoting without pushing ideologies down people's throats.

Leaders can't effectively inspire positive social impact among their followers without resisting, protesting, or rebelling against wrong, widely held notions.

Mental Health and Well-Being in Leadership

Whenever you find yourself in an emergency while on-board an aircraft, flight attendants would tell you to 'put your oxygen mask on first, before helping others.'

Now, you don't ask, 'What if I'm with my girlfriend whom I love so much, and she's finding it hard to put on the mask?'

Well, you should put on your oxygen mask first, or both you and your girlfriend might pay for your self-neglect because you went out of oxygen during the struggle.

Research has shown that leaders today suffer from poor well-being and mental health challenges more than ever before.

If that isn't inspiring enough, further unconnected research has proven that younger people today have more chances of suffering from mental breakdowns and other psychological issues than older folks.

Caring for your mental health and well-being is important for yourself, as well as for inspiring your followers toward healthier lifestyles.

As a leader, it's your job to demonstrate what success should look like to your team members.

Of course, you don't have to be a perfectly successful leader. But success without health or proper well-being is not worth emulating.

You might find various tips online on other materials on maintaining positive well-being or improved mental health as a leader. Sadly, they're sometimes disparaging and can be too much to take in at once.

On the other hand, how about you create daily habits to feel reassured about maintaining proper mental health and overall well-being as a leader?

Start Every Day with a Routine

There's no overestimating the power of daily routines – if you follow them – in helping you take on amazing leadership qualities.

First, your morning is very important because it sets the pace for the rest of your day. You want to create a morning routine that gives you more control of your day.

Additionally, you want to create a schedule that includes ideas to improve your health, mood, energy levels, and the ability to concentrate at work.

You want to set aside as little time as possible, say 30 minutes, for your routine. That way, you can maintain your routine and hopefully expand it with time.

Then, look out for the health and wellness goals you intend to practice. It could include meditation, exercising, listening to music, or taking a cold shower.

You might want to keep your phone or gadgets on airplane mode or away to avoid distractions or getting pulled from work.

Ethical Leadership in the Business World

Ethical leadership isn't just needed in advocating social values or running a not-for-profit. It's also necessary even in for-profit brands and activities.

As I've explained earlier, ethical leadership involves highlighting your core values and staying bold enough to live them out. However, in this case, the subject is your business or for-profit brand.

I've covered what ethical leadership means in the previous chapter and wouldn't bore you by repeating its ideals (ethics are primarily the same for both businesses and personal brands).

However, how about I show you why or how your business can profit from ethical leadership in a highly profit-driven world?

How Your Business Can Profit from Ethical Leadership

1. **Evokes Confidence in Potential Investors**

Potential investors are likely to express more confidence in your brand when they know you're ethically doing business.

2. **Builds Customer Loyalty**

What people think about your organization's morality can break or make your brand identity. Various research has shown over the years that consumers are more likely to patronize a brand that includes CSR in its activities.

If you're deliberate about being ethical in your business, word will soon get around that your brand has good intentions to improve the world.

3. **Good Social Proof**

When a brand practices moral misconduct to a level, the public soon learns about it, and its image gets smeared. Avoid ruining your brand's good name by engaging in immoral activities.

4. **Establish Trust from Partners**

Your partners are likely to believe and trust you when they discover you have ethical standards you uphold.

Plus, you'd likely attract brands, businesses, and partners who uphold similar values, potentially building a reliable foundation of mutual respect and trust.

On the flip side, attracting other immoral partners or vendors will only complicate your situation and won't end well for your brand.

5. **Maintain a High Morale that Boosts Performance**

As Accenture's research proves in the last chapter on ethical leadership, building your business on ethics can increase your chances of boosting your organization's earnings.

There are various reasons why Accenture succeeded after including more disabled people in their staff role. However, research showed that Gen Z is happier working in organizations that uphold social causes or practice CSR.

Maintaining ethics in your business will make your team members proud of your brand and possibly boost their morale while on the job.

Leading through Uncertainty: Strategies for Navigating Ambiguity and Ambivalence

When I was younger and in high school, I had to lead a team of other students during a period of intense uncertainty about the group's future.

While our fears about a negative change lasted, I applied some strategies I'll show you shortly to keep the group in shape. Fortunately, normalcy returned to the group, and our fears were proved wrong.

3 Basic Strategies for Navigating Uncertainty as a Leader

- **Keep Communication Lines Open and Transparent**

Maintaining open and transparent communication lines with your team becomes crucial during seasons where ambivalence and ambiguity abound.

During the season I highlighted earlier, I told all I knew about the situation, providing necessary updates on developments relating to the situation as they arose.

Transparent communications foster trust and a shared sense of purpose, making the season more bearable (or enjoyable).

- **Offer Clarity and Direction**

Your team needs to know what direction you're possibly leading them. Uncertainty can create confusion and anxiety in the organization. You want to break down the (potential) issues involved in the season and outline a roadmap to guide your followers through the moments.

Doing this will, among other things, enshrine confidence in your team, helping them concentrate on what needs to be done at a time.

- **Support and Empower Your Group**

Transition seasons or seasons of high uncertainty require a new set of skills or opportunities for collaboration.

During seasons of ambiguity, support and empower your team by providing adequate training, coaching, and resources to develop new capabilities and adapt to current ones.

That said, don't hesitate to encourage high-performing team members while pushing others to improve their contributions to the team's overall goals.

During my team's 'transition period,' I achieved this by maintaining a clear goal for the team to follow and insisting on it. That way, discouraged team members could readily find courage in my stance and hold on in good faith.

Empowering Future Generations

An Ernst & Young survey finds that Gen Z and Gen Alpha understand sustainability issues more deeply than others. Intriguingly, the survey says Gen Z and Gen Alpha sustain high eagerness to learn more about the topic.

Gen Z complained that the education received in school on sustainability was superficial, outdated, and uninspiring. To them, the best platforms to foster improvements are workshops and hands-on learning opportunities.

Now, if you're still wondering what these have to do with you as a leader who intends to positively influence the world around you, here's it.

The only way to feed a malnourished population is by feeding them. And if Gen Z feel they're highly malnourished or empowered to face the realities of their world, how much more will future generations?

The 21st-century leader will do well to harness the potential of younger generations toward lending their voice to their preferred social cause. And one way to achieve this is by raising the environmental and social literacy of the younger folks.

While schools will do great to contribute their quota in educating the upcoming generation, you don't want to leave this to them alone.

Meanwhile, by consistently educating younger folks on issues of global interest, you position them to understand better what they learned in school about similar subjects.

They're also likely to express more freedom outside the four walls of the classroom in hands-on and practical classes with no 'school ground rules' or undercover grades behind them.

Building a Legacy

Now, wait!

You don't have to wait until you're in your 50s or 60s before considering a legacy to pass on to others.

'Legacy', like Dan Rockwell, a leadership commentator, says, 'is about life, not death.'

Building a legacy is the only way to leave a lasting footprint behind you. It's the summary of others' experience of your leadership. It's the reward of your leadership actions that (*should*) forever improve the world around you.

Even more, leaving a legacy is the only way to help the younger ones feel part of a cause that's greater than themselves. A legacy shows them that previous generations have sacrificed for them, invested in them, and charted a course for them.

However, you only leave a worthwhile legacy when you consciously work in a way that builds one.

So, how do you build a lasting legacy that's neither difficult to destroy nor erase as a leader? Remember, my focus here is building a worthy and *positive* legacy behind you.

Define What Legacy Means to You

Whether it's being remembered for promoting timeliness, dedication, respect for elders, or female education, you start building your legacy by defining what you want to leave behind you.

Do you intend to build on the legacy of your role models or mentors? Or are you interested in carving a new legacy niche for yourself? Decide what you want to be known for when you're out of leadership, and you have a course to chart.

Anchor Your Legacy on Something You Love

Anchor your legacy on your strengths. You don't want to build or pursue a legacy that feels like a chore.

What do people say are your strengths? What have past team leads or mentors complimented about your contribution to the environment? These can tell a great deal about subjects you can cornerstone your legacy on.

Also, check out topics and values you're passionate about. The stories you find compelling or interesting can help you find where your heart rests and possibly inform your legacy ideas.

Write Your Legacy in a Simple Sentence

One way to establish focus and concentration is by summarizing your legacy in a simple sentence. You only need to overcome one little hurdle: eliminate all unnecessary goals and close in on the must-dos of your life's goals.

Summarizing your legacy in one sentence can help you clarify your mission and pursue it with an unstoppable focus.

Spend Your Time Wisely Living Your Legacy

Once you have an action plan, you're ready to implement it.

You want to consider possible actions and plans to help you live your legacy to the fullest. It's also important to align yourself with people who can help build, inspire, or contribute to your legacy.

Meanwhile, what if you choose not to consciously build a legacy for others behind you? Well, that would be impossible because legacy sums up all you're leaving behind for future generations.

Leaving a Positive Impact and Inspiring Future Generations

This book highlights ways to leave a positive social impact and inspire future generations to do the same.

However, having read through this, you may wonder where to start.

I show you four easy ways to give back to make a positive impact, improve your community, and start leaving a good legacy now.

1. **Donate Supplies**

Clothing, food, clothing, blood, and more are some of the best things you can give to your community.

Remember children, the elderly, and other less-privileged communities while doing this. Contact the local school board, heads of schools, and foster homes in your district and speak to them about donating supplies.

2. **Mentor Someone**

Mentoring doesn't just impact your mentees but you as well. That's because you'd get to hone your best skills, develop talent in your field, and create a lasting legacy.

Now, you don't need to accomplish everything your heart wishes for before accepting to mentor someone. There are younger and less experienced folks around you who have fewer resources and need education in your field.

Find ways to teach and introduce them to your strengths, skills, and opportunities. Research platforms and organizations that allow you to provide mentorship to children who need positive role models and mentors.

There's no overestimating the impact you can have by supporting a child via focused mentorship.

3. **Volunteer**

There are no limits to the ways you can volunteer. Do you love animals and care about their welfare? Volunteer at an animal shelter.

Do you want older people to be less lonely? Volunteer to spend some time in older people's homes. Are you passionate about girl-child education in developing countries? How about joining to raise funds for that cause?

Volunteering also includes running errands for elderly residents in your neighborhood or picking up groceries for others during your routine shopping rounds.

4. **Pick up Trash**

Picking up trash in school or the neighborhood shows that you care about and take pride in your neighborhood. It also makes people around you feel more comfortable in the area.

Whether it's a yard that needs some sprucing up or calling a team of other students to clean up the dining room in real time, clearing waste in the environment can help you make a positive impact around you.

There are many other ways to show you care for your environment and others, positively impact them, and leave a positive legacy behind you. You could begin with only one act of giving back before increasing your web of kindness to include other activities.

Soon, you'll have a cascade of actions that can jumpstart your team into one that makes never-ending contributions to improve the world.

Maintaining a Healthy Relationship with Technology

I've emphasized why you need to be a compassionate tech-savvy leader who inspires others to maximize 21st-century opportunities to solve 21st-century challenges.

But younger people often get into the trap of overusing or over-relying on technology to achieve their goals.

If you asked me, I think every gadget you own should bear a sticker bearing these two words:

'Use Responsibly.'

Leadership in a Changing World

50% of tech users will click on a notification within 30 seconds of receiving it. If they don't view it, their chances of opening it drop to 17%.

Meanwhile, research by the National Center for Biotechnology Information (NCBI) shows that too much tech can impair your satisfaction with relationships, cause physiological damage, and could have adverse health effects.

Creating media boundaries can help reduce excessive dependence on technology, putting you on the right path to a healthier use of technology.

How do you set responsible boundaries for using technology? How do you maintain tech hygiene even though 65% of your brand's activities require some form of technology to pass?

Here are three technological best practices to foster a healthier relationship with technology.

1. Reduce Phone Time

Many people would check their phones first thing in the morning. But that couldn't be far from proper tech hygiene.

Avoid rushing to your phone early to avoid spending your most productive hours in the morning doing anything other than what you intend to do during the day.

Set rules to limit screen time and create boundaries between your personal and professional life. That way, you can easily shut off from work and fully recharge to focus on building better relationships with friends and loved ones.

2. If possible, Schedule Incoming Notifications with a Software

Find software that collates all your messages and delivers them at an exclusive time of the day. Avoid getting thrown off your day's schedule by an insignificant email that requires only two minutes of your time (that could become two hours in a zap!).

Consider dedicating a few times of the day to viewing notifications and emails. Doing so can help avoid shifting your attention away from crucial tasks whenever a notification rings over your device.

Considering useful software to use here? Have you heard of 7shifts? Connecteam? Jobber? Wrike. When I Work?

There are scores of them.

3. **Take Breaks and Stay Away from Technology Every Couple of Hours**

Taking a break from your gadgets can help you rejuvenate and stay healthier. Meanwhile, you want to reduce the brightness of the LCD or change your screen to black and white so your eyes and brain can relax during long working hours.

Take regular breaks from the desk. Take a walk outside or propose a tea break that lets team members know one another better. Additionally, taking valuable and short breaks can help your mind refresh and perform better when you're back at the desk.

Workbook 9

The 21-Day Legacy Challenge

You have a challenge before you.

Remember the sections on leaving a lasting and *positive* legacy for younger generations? Here's an exciting way to begin.

I've compiled a skeletal framework outlining a 21-day schedule of how you'll work toward living a legacy for others behind you.

Feel free to tweak its contents, but here's just a guide to help you master the art of working toward – and building – a legacy you'll be proud of when the curtain is drawn on your leadership.

Day 1 – Re-Read this chapter, paying attention to sections that talk about building a lasting legacy.

Day 2 – What do you want to be remembered for? Decide what you want to be remembered for.

Day 3 – Via online research, library searches, and speaking with others, search for Past Leaders who have built a legacy similar to yours.

Day 4 – Study the activities and lifestyle of your new role models – people who have left or are building a legacy similar to your proposed legacy.

Day 5 – Identify your strengths. Speak with family, friends, partners, and mentors about what they think you know how to do best.

Day 6 – Check whether your strengths align with your legacy. Note any lapses or weaknesses in your character that could impair your building your desired legacy.

Day 7 – Create a plan or strategy to beat or reduce the potential impact of your weaknesses on building your favorite legacy. That could include outlining partners to work with or learning new skills.

Day 8 – Write a 400-word essay about what you want to be remembered for

Day 9 – Reduce your 400-word essay into a paragraph, eliminating unnecessaries in the 400-word essay you wrote on Day 8. Ensure the final paragraph holds only the most important indices you want to be mirrored in your memoir.

Day 10 – Now, reduce that final paragraph to a simple line. It might be hard. But find a way to get it done. Only ensure you aren't leaving any vital aspects out in the bid to create a simple sentence. Also, avoid the temptation to create a fuzzy or *woke* legacy line. Just keep it simple.

Day 11 – Speak to a mentor (or trusted older person) about your desired legacy. Ask for their ideas or advice on it. Ask trusted people around you (friends, colleagues, family, etc.) what they think about your legacy line or if it needs a little tweaking.

Day 12 – Break Down Your Legacy into Four Actions, like those I recommended in the section, *Leaving a Positive Impact and Inspiring Future Generations.* Letter each action A, B, C, and D. So, for instance, A could pick up trash. Take some time to Plan Action A

Day 13 – Execute Action A

Day 14 – Take a break to review Day 13. What were the challenges you faced while trying to execute action A? What did you enjoy about it? Would you like to do this more often? Plan against Action B

Day 15 – Execute Action B

Day 16 – Review Day 15. What were the challenges you faced while trying to execute action A? What did you enjoy about it? Identify if you would like to do this more often. Plan against Action C

Day 17 – Execute Action C

Day 18 - Review Day 17. What were the challenges you faced while trying to execute action A? What did you enjoy about it? Identify if you would like to do this more often. Plan against Action D

Day 19 – Execute Action D

Day 20 – Review Day 19. What were the challenges you faced while trying to execute action A? What did you enjoy about it? Identify if you would like to do this more often.

Day 21 – Review your performance in the entire challenge. Would you like to retake the challenge?

Exercise

Speak to at least one team member or one other person about your 21-day challenge. Tell them why building a legacy is important and why they should take on a similar challenge.

Takeaway 9

Whether you want to be a leader of global influence or otherwise, you already *potentially* are.

The futuristic leader will invest enough resources into educating valuable subjects to the younger generations in more engaging ways.

BONUS SECTION: TEN EXTRAORDINARY TEEN LEADERS TO GLEAN FROM

Malala Yousafzai

It's pretty mind-blowing how someone's life story can light up the way for others. Let me introduce you to a true teen leader who's not just shining a light but igniting a beacon of hope for millions. Her name is Malala Yousafzai, and her journey is nothing short of incredible.

Born in Mingora, Pakistan, on July 12, 1997, Malala's story began in a place where girls' education wasn't always celebrated. But her father, Ziauddin Yousafzai, believed in giving her every opportunity, just like a boy would have. He was a teacher who ran a girls' school in their village, planting a strong desire for learning in her young mind.

Imagine how everything changed when the Taliban took control of their town. They banned girls from going to school, enforcing harsh rules. But even in the face of darkness, Malala's light shone brightly. When the threats against her life increased, she had to say goodbye to classmates at just eleven, not knowing if she'd ever see them again.

And then, something incredible happened. Malala spoke out for girls' right to learn. That simple act made her a target. In 2012, a gunman boarded her school bus, asking, "Who is Malala?" He shot her, hoping to silence her voice, but instead, he ignited a global movement.

After ten days of struggling for her life, Malala's tenacity brought her to a hospital in England, where she eventually woke up. She realized she had a choice: she could remain silent, or, with her family's support, she could use the second chance she had been given.

And boy, did she choose the latter.

Alongside her father, Malala founded the Malala Fund, a charity that's all about giving girls the power of education. Her path wasn't straightforward; it was filled with obstacles and determination. She received the Nobel Peace Prize in 2014 for her tenacious fight, making her the world's youngest-ever laureate at age 17.

Malala later went to Oxford University, majoring in economics, politics, and philosophy. But she didn't stop there.

She traveled the world, meeting girls fighting against adversity to go to school. Like her father, she invested in activists and educators through Malala Fund's Education Champion Network.

Now, as an Oxford graduate, Malala's mission continues. She knows that more work must be done because over 130 million girls are not in school.

Here's the thing, my friend – Malala's story teaches us so much about leadership. She showed us that standing up for what's right, even in the face of danger, is what leaders do. She exhibited resilience, determination, and the power of using her voice to make change happen.

Leadership in a Changing World

Greta Thunberg

Greta Thunberg's name has become synonymous with climate activism in most places around the world. Born on January 3, 2003, in Stockholm, Sweden, Greta didn't wait until she was an adult to start changing the world.

She was a teenager, sparking a global movement to combat climate change. That's incredible, right? But what's even more amazing is the event that made her care about the environment that much.

Greta's story starts with her parents – an opera singer mom and an actor dad. She was diagnosed with Asperger's syndrome, a form of autism that makes Greta see the world uniquely. She embraced her passion for the environment and founded Fridays for Future, a movement that turned skipping school into a powerful protest for climate action.

Imagine her sitting alone outside the Swedish parliament, holding a sign that said, "School Strike for Climate." That lone protest ignited a fire. Students worldwide joined her, skipping school on Fridays to demand action on climate change. Greta's courage sparked the "Greta effect," inspiring millions to raise their voices for the planet.

With determination, she addressed world leaders at the United Nations, holding them accountable for their empty promises. Her passion was evident in her words: "How dare you!" she challenged, demanding action against the threat of the climate crisis.

Greta wasn't just a voice for the environment; she was a symbol of strength for those with Asperger's. She proved that being different could be a superpower. Through her speeches and books, like "No One Is Too Small to Make a Difference," she educated the world about climate change and her own condition.

What strikes me about Greta's story is her fearlessness. She didn't let age hold her back. She demonstrated unwavering tenacity, the strength of a lone voice, and the guts to stand up for what is right. Greta's actions serve as a reminder that even one person—especially a young person—can influence the world in a society when many people choose to remain silent.

Boyan Slat

Let's explore the life of Boyan Slat, a trailblazing teenager making waves of change in our oceans. Born with an innate curiosity and drive, Boyan's story began when he went diving in 2011 and discovered something alarming – there was more plastic in the water than fish. This shocking realization ignited his determination to combat plastic pollution and its impact on marine life.

Boyan's leadership story started in high school, when he went diving, only to discover that the plastic waste seemed to be more than fish in his diving area. He decided to take on the seemingly insurmountable task of ocean cleanup using the high school project he was working on to provide a sustainable solution to this environmental problem rather than merely shrugging his shoulders. His idea was simple yet revolutionary: a passive plastic catchment system that harnessed ocean currents to collect plastic waste. This idea took shape in 2012 when he gave a TEDx talk, sparking widespread attention.

Boyan is a unique leader because he believes in the endless possibilities of technology. "Technology is the most potent agent of change," he declared. He understood that innovation may produce fresh answers to challenging issues, so he decided to put his understanding into practice. In 2013, he established The Ocean Cleanup, a nonprofit organization devoted to cleaning up plastic garbage from our seas.

But Boyan's journey wasn't all smooth sailing. He faced challenges and technical failures, like the first systems that encountered issues capturing plastic. Yet, he persisted and improved, showcasing resilience and adaptability – key leadership traits.

Boyan's innovation didn't stop there. He unveiled The Interceptor, a solar-powered barge-like system designed to collect plastic from the world's most polluted rivers. His goal was to "close the tap" on plastic entering the oceans, highlighting his forward-thinking approach and commitment to sustainable solutions.

Throughout his journey, Boyan received recognition and awards for his exceptional leadership. He proved that age is just a number for making a positive impact. Boyan's story teaches us that leadership involves turning ideas into action, persisting through challenges, and using innovation to shape a better future.

Maya Penn

Maya Penn is a powerhouse teen entrepreneur, shaping the world with her creativity and determination. Maya, born on February 10, 2000, in Atlanta, is a living example of the difference one can make, even while still young.

She started her business, Maya's Ideas, an eco-friendly fashion company, when she was eight. Her leadership journey began with a passion for making a difference. Maya's commitment to sustainability and artistry led her to create clothing that's stylish and kind to the planet. It's a reminder that your passions can drive you to do extraordinary things.

Maya's talents don't stop at fashion. She's an animator and artist, bringing her creativity to life through animated series like "The Pollinators." Through her art, she highlights the importance of bees and other pollinators, showcasing her leadership in raising awareness about critical environmental issues.

But Maya's leadership isn't limited to her artistic endeavors. She's a force for change in the world. She's actively supported One Billion Rising and Girls, Inc., showing that leadership isn't just about leading a company – it's about supporting and lifting others.

In 2011, Maya took her commitment to the next level by founding her own nonprofit, Maya's Ideas 4 The Planet. Her dedication to making the world a better place earned her a spot on Oprah's SuperSoul 100 list of visionaries and influential leaders. She serves as a reminder that getting things done is not age-related.

Maya's narrative is about more than simply her accomplishments; it's also about the leadership qualities that come through. Her devotion to the causes she supports and her love for them demonstrates the sort of leadership that can transform the world. Maya reminds us that we can start making a difference right now, no matter our age.

Xiuhtezcatl Martinez

Xiuhtezcatl Roske-Martinez is a young environmental activist and hip-hop artist who has been making waves in the world since his teenage years. Imagine this: Xiuhtezcatl, also known as X, was just like any other teenager, navigating life's challenges but with a unique twist. He chose to channel his passion for change into a powerful force for good.

Born in Colorado and deeply connected to his Aztec heritage, Xiuhtezcatl's journey began when he realized the profound impact of climate change on indigenous and marginalized communities. Can you picture addressing the UN and fervently emphasizing the dire necessity for action in light of the effects of fossil fuels? That's exactly what 15-year-old Xiuhtezcatl accomplished, making a speech that was well-received in English and Spanish and in his native Nahuatl.

What truly sets Xiuhtezcatl apart is his unshakable commitment to his convictions. Not only is he calling for reform, but he has also filed a lawsuit against the United States. In the Juliana v. United States case, Xiuhtezcatl is one of the main plaintiffs. He is suing the government of the United States for failing to address climate change, claiming that this violates his generation's constitutional rights.

But Xiuhtezcatl doesn't stop there. He is also a key influence behind Earth Guardians, a group that equips young people to lead initiatives for social justice and the environment. Can you imagine organizing climate strikes, advocating for policy changes, and inspiring others through art, music, and storytelling? Xiuhtezcatl is doing just that.

His journey reminds us that every voice matters, regardless of age. Xiuhtezcatl's leadership showcases that young people have the power to drive change and create a better world, even when faced with challenges. So, as you navigate your own path, remember that your passion, dedication, and commitment can lead to extraordinary impact.

Akilah Johnson

Let's step into the world of Akilah Johnson, a remarkable teenager who shattered barriers and showcased the power of embracing her unique identity. Picture this: Akilah, a sophomore in high school, used her artistic talents to create a Google Doodle that celebrated her Afrocentric heritage. Can you imagine seeing your artwork on the Google homepage for millions to see, representing your culture and identity?

Akilah's masterpiece, titled "My Afrocentric Life," beautifully captured the essence of Black culture and history. Her doodle featured a vibrant young Afro woman surrounded by symbols of Black origin, weaving together past and present history and identity. This doodle was a celebration of being unashamedly Black and more than simply art.

Akilah's leadership shines through her commitment to showcasing her true self. In a world that sometimes asks us to conform, she boldly embraced her roots and let her culture be her guide. She explained that her school shaped her Afrocentric lifestyle, which emphasized a strong connection to African heritage. As she put it, "I learned a lot about my history as an African American." Can you feel the strength in her words?

But Akilah's impact went beyond her artwork. She's the first African American to win Google's Doodle 4 Google competition, standing out among 100,000 submissions. Her doodle celebrated her heritage and highlighted iconic figures like Nelson Mandela and Rosa Parks, weaving them into her artistic narrative.

Akilah's story teaches us that embracing our identity and culture is a form of leadership. It's about speaking up for who we are, unapologetically and proudly. Her courage to stand out and be true to herself led to history-making recognition.

Jack Andraka

Jack Thomas Andraka is a young genius who shook up the world with his groundbreaking work. Jack was just like any other high school student. He took on the challenge of creating a sensor that could detect the early stages of pancreatic cancer. As it turned out, his sensor, like those diabetic test strips, could potentially save lives by catching cancer early.

Now, picture Jack working tirelessly on his project, using filter paper coated with tiny carbon nanotubes and special antibodies. These little warriors could measure a substance called mesothelin, giving a hint if cancer were lurking. His project was a hit, winning the prestigious Gordon E. Moore Award at the Intel International Science and Engineering Fair.

But here's the thing – Jack's journey wasn't all smooth sailing. People questioned his method, saying it didn't make scientific sense. Some experts doubted his claims about speed and accuracy. Yet, Jack's determination shone through. He stood by his work and applied for a patent, ready to take on the doubters.

Here's where Jack's leadership traits shine. Despite the naysayers, he stood his ground and believed in his idea. He used his passion to make a difference, even though he faced skepticism. Jack's story teaches us that leaders don't give up when faced with obstacles; instead, they believe in their vision and work hard to make it a reality. Therefore, keep in mind that even as a teen, you have the power to change the world with your ideas. But that would mean you cannot afford to give up. You must fight for your dream. It might potentially save a lot of other people in the future.

Leadership in a Changing World

Zuriel Oduwole

Zuriel's story is like a blockbuster movie – full of passion, determination, and world-changing moments. She's a young trailblazer changing the world with her inspiring leadership. Zuriel burst onto the scene as a true education advocate and filmmaker. She's like a superhero for girls' education in Africa. Did you know she made her first documentary when she was only ten? That's like fifth grade! Her films are like a magic potion – they spread awareness about the importance of education for girls in Africa.

But wait, it gets even cooler. She's not just making movies; she's meeting presidents and prime ministers! She regularly talks to world leaders about the importance of education. Zuriel met more than world leaders in her little time here on Earth. She's been on major channels like CNBC, Bloomberg TV, BBC, and CNN. Yep, she's basically famous!

Zuriel is on a mission and has awards to prove it. She's been listed in magazines like Forbes, Elle, and The New York Times. It's like her room is a trophy cabinet! She even won the Ban Ki-moon leadership award – you know, the former United Nations Secretary-General?

One of the coolest things she's done is creating her own awards for first ladies and gender ministers. It's like she's giving out golden stars to these leaders for helping girls get an education.

Zuriel's not just talking; she's taking action. She's teaching filmmaking to girls who don't have access to traditional schools. It's like she's handing out superpowers! And she's fighting against girl marriage – she's a real-life superhero protecting girls' futures.

Did you know that she is from California, too? Yes, she embodies the big-dreaming, change-making Californian attitude. She even produced a film to inspire young people to participate in determining the course of their state's destiny.

So, what can we learn from Zuriel? She's like a wise big sister, showing the world that young folks could positively contribute to the development of their immediate environment and the world at large. Her story is proof that you don't need a cape to be a hero – just passion, determination, and a heart full of courage.

Alex Lin

It's pretty amazing how one teenager can make a massive difference in the world. Imagine being just 11 years old and stumbling upon a news article about the piles of electronic waste, or E-waste, that nobody cared about. That's what happened to Alex Lin from Westerly, Rhode Island. He saw a problem that everyone else ignored – the pollution caused by throwing away old electronics like computers and phones.

Alex didn't just shrug it off. Nope, he did something about it. He got together with his friends and formed a group called W.I.N – Westerly Innovations Network. Their goal? To recycle E-waste and give access to technology for kids in poorer countries. Can you believe they transformed a whopping 300,000 pounds of E-waste into new computers for places like Cameroon and Sierra?

But guess what? They didn't stop there. Alex and his team wanted to change things at a bigger level. They worked to ban E-waste dumping in Rhode Island. Imagine how much courage that took! They faced setbacks and disappointments, but they kept pushing forward. They rallied people with fliers, articles, and presentations. Eventually, their hard work paid off, and Rhode Island passed a law against E-waste dumping.

You might be thinking, "Why does this matter to me?" Well, it's about using your voice and power to make the world better. Being a teen activist is simply standing up for what's right, just like Alex Lin did.

So, my friend, remember Alex Lin's story. This is not just about him; it's actually about you. There are leadership traits you can learn from him that could help make you a better leader. Traits like courage, determination, and the belief that even one teenager can create a massive impact. You've got the power to change the world, too, even if you're not a grown-up yet. Keep your eyes open for problems around you, gather your friends just like Alex did, and make some noise for what's right.

Ryan Hickman

Ryan Hickman was just three years old when he discovered the magic of recycling. He went to a recycling center with his dad, turned in some cans and bottles, and realized that recycling was his calling. Can you believe it?

The next day, he had a brilliant idea. He asked his neighbors if they'd save their recyclables for him, and guess what? Not only did his neighbors join in, but their friends, families, and co-workers joined the recycling mission, too! Ryan's passion for recycling was like wildfire, spreading all over Orange County, CA.

Here's where the leadership magic comes in: Ryan showed us that even a young person can be a change-maker. His determination and courage to take action is mind-blowing. He didn't stop at just collecting recyclables. Nope! He set a big goal – to stop cans and bottles from harming our oceans, which marine life calls home. Week after week, he sorted through stacks of recyclables, getting them ready for the recycling center.

Ryan's story went viral in 2016, and he became a worldwide sensation! He's been on TV shows like Ellen DeGeneres, inspiring millions with his recycling journey. He's spoken at WE DAY events and even snagged awards like the "Citizen of the Year" in his hometown. His recycling story has also been featured on major platforms like CNN, NBC, and National Geographic. How cool is that?

Ryan's not just a recycling superstar; he's an environmental educator, too! He speaks at schools and events, spreading his passion for a greener world.

Conclusion

A few centuries ago, the West celebrated the rise of the Industrial Revolution. Top management executives in factories reveled in their ability to compel or 'motivate' their employees to work harder and produce more.

When brutal force wasn't the tool (like during the Slave Trade), improved working conditions and commissions were the bait.

However, the Digital Age has demonstrated that industrial-age thinking isn't sufficient to drive the innovation and creativity that births modern development in the 21st century.

What the world needs today, more than ever, are empathetic leaders who understand how to leverage Information Technology to steer a team in the right direction.

If you've read this book to this point, congratulations!

You've learned the most valuable leadership qualities to impact today's world positively.

But you didn't learn just that. I've also shown you how to develop your unique leadership style, whether or not you're already leading others. While building a worthwhile and emulative character is great for creating a great profile – and recommended in this book – you also want to offer and effectively communicate value to your followers.

Conclusion

Afterward, I lasered down on fostering team unity and collaborativeness while being resilient about growth. But beyond leading with resilience and meeting performance metrics, I've *almost screamed* about how critical ethical leadership is to your ultimate success.

Fortunately, ethical leadership is more achievable than it might appear. And I've shown you just how to build an ethical brand.

Google has topped Fortune's list of 'Best Company to Work For' six consecutive times. The American tech giant ensures its team members share common goals. Even more, it strives to maintain a diverse team that reflects its global audience while maintaining an open culture where everyone feels free to air their opinions.

Google's story mirrors, to a large extent, the leadership qualities this book has extolled and presented.

I leave you with a favorite quote from Arthur Ashe:

Start where you are. Use what you have. Do what you can.

Now, I want to ask you a favor. Fortunately, it aligns with one of the tenets of good leadership: sharing helpful information with others.

If you enjoyed this book, kindly leave it a review on Amazon, inviting others to benefit as you have.

See you at the top, champ!

References

Mateja. (2021). 7 Youth Leadership Statistics Including Influence On Community 2022. OfficeNeedle. https://officeneedle.com/youth-leadership-statistics/

Bhatia, K., Rath, S., Pradhan, H., Samal, S., Copas, A., Gagrai, S., Rath, S., Gope, R. K., Nair, N., Tripathy, P., Rose-Clarke, K., & Prost, A. (2023). Effects of community youth teams facilitating participatory adolescent groups, youth leadership activities and livelihood promotion to improve school attendance, dietary diversity and mental health among adolescent girls in rural eastern India (JIAH trial): A cluster-randomized controlled trial. SSM-Population Health, 21, 101330. https://doi.org/10.1016/j.ssmph.2022.101330

Locke, E. A., & Latham, G. P. (2006). New directions in goal-setting theory. Current Directions in Psychological Science, 15(5), 265-268.

Eby, L. T., Allen, T. D., Evans, S. C., Ng, T., & DuBois, D. L. (2008). Does mentoring matter? A multidisciplinary meta-analysis comparing mentored and non-mentored individuals. Journal of Vocational Behavior, 72(2), 254-267.

Kluger, A. N., & DeNisi, A. (1996). The effects of feedback interventions on performance: A historical review, a meta-analysis, and a preliminary feedback intervention theory. Psychological Bulletin, 119(2), 254-284.

Ragins, B. R., & Verbos, A. K. (2007). Positive relationships in action: Relational mentoring and mentoring schemas in the workplace. In Positive organizational scholarship (pp. 149-167). Routledge.

Dweck, C. S. (2016). Mindset: The New Psychology of Success. Random House.

MENTOR. (2020). The Mentoring Effect. National Mentoring Partnership.

References

Johnson, C. E. (2019). Meeting the ethical challenges of leadership: Casting light or shadow (6th ed.). SAGE Publications.

Dirks, K. T., & Ferrin, D. L. (2002). Trust in leadership: Meta-analytic findings and implications for research and practice. Journal of Applied Psychology, 87(4), 611-628.

Smith, A., & Johnson, M. (2020). Responsibility and Goal Achievement: A Correlational Study. Journal of Personal Growth, 16(2), 45-62.

Brown, G., Williams, R., & Martinez, L. (2018). Fostering Accountability in Teams: Effects on Engagement and Performance. Group Dynamics, 22(3), 167-183

Smith, A. N., Jones, J. M., Khazanchi, S., & Johnson, D. E. (2020). The Positive Effects of Humility and Servant Leadership on Leader Effectiveness. Journal of Leadership & Organizational Studies, 27(3), 252-266.

Owens, B. P., Johnson, M. D., & Mitchell, T. R. (2013). Expressed Humility in Organizations: Implications for Performance, Teams, and Leadership. Organization Science, 24(5), 1517-1538.

Liden, R. C., Wayne, S. J., Liao, C., & Meuser, J. D. (2014). Servant Leadership and Serving Culture: Influence on Individual and Unit Performance. Academy of Management Journal, 57(5), 1434-1452.

Levine, J. M., & Moreland, R. L. (2014). Diversity makes better: A response to three common criticisms of diversity. Psychological Inquiry, 25(1), 46-55.

Gudykunst, W. B., & Kim, Y. Y. (2005). Communicating with strangers: An approach to intercultural communication. McGraw-Hill.

Johnson, D. W., & Johnson, R. T. (2013). Joining Together: Group Theory and Group Skills. Pearson.

Southwick, S. M., & Charney, D. S. (2018). Resilience: The science of mastering life's greatest challenges. Cambridge University Press.

Bonanno, G. A. (2004). Loss, trauma, and human resilience: Have we underestimated the human capacity to thrive after extremely aversive events? American Psychologist, 59(1), 20-28.

Keller, A., Litzelman, K., Wisk, L. E., Maddox, T., Cheng, E. R., Creswell, P. D., & Witt, W. P. (2012). Does the perception that stress affects health matter? The association with health and mortality. Health Psychology, 31(5), 677-684

Carney, D. R., Cuddy, A. J., & Yap, A. J. (2010). Power Posing: Brief Nonverbal Displays Affect Neuroendocrine Levels and Risk Tolerance. Psychological Science, 21(10), 1363–1368.

Smith, E. R., & Wigley, S. (2020). The importance of active listening: Recognizing the essential role of the listener. The Journal of Positive Psychology, 15(2), 153-160.

Brown, K. W., & Ryan, R. M. (2003). The benefits of being present: Mindfulness and its role in psychological well-being. Journal of Personality and Social Psychology, 84(4), 822-848.

Eisenberger, R., Huntington, R., Hutchison, S., & Sowa, D. (2002). Perceived organizational support. Journal of Applied Psychology, 87(4), 698-714.

Paulus, P. B., & Brown, V. R. (2003). Enhancing ideational creativity in groups: Lessons from research on brainstorming. Group Dynamics: Theory, Research, and Practice, 7(13), 110-123.

Nadler, R. T., Nir, D., & Kurland, N. B. (2009). The impact of question structure on the quality of responses to open questions. Organizational Research Methods, 12(2), 241-258.

Guttman, H. M. (2004). The role of conflict resolution in leadership effectiveness. The Health Care Manager, 23(4), 334-339.

Zhang, X., Cao, J., & Tjosvold, D. (2011). Linking transformational leadership and team performance: A conflict management approach. Journal of Applied Psychology, 96(4), 771-781.

Citroen, C. L. (2011). The role of information in strategic decision-making. *International journal of information management*, *31*(6), 493-501.

Clausen, K. W. (2016). ACTION: EQUAL & OPPOSITE. *The Canadian Journal of Action Research*, 17(1), 1.

Cook, B. (2023). The ultimate guide to collaborative decision making. *Fellow.app*. https://fellow.app/blog/management/the-ultimate-guide-to-collaborative-decision-making/

References

Bivins, T. H. (2006). Responsibility and accountability. Ethics in public relations: Responsible advocacy, 19-38.

Brophy, D. R. (1998). Understanding, measuring, and enhancing individual creative problem-solving efforts. *Creativity Research Journal*, 11(2), 123-150.

Erikson, R. (2006). Social class assignment and mortality in Sweden. *Social science & medicine*, *62*(9), 2151-2160.

Forsey, C. (2018, August 22). How to Practice Ethical Decision Making at Work. *Hubspot*. Retrieved August 17, 2023, from https://blog.hubspot.com/marketing/ethical-decision-making

Fritzsche, D. J. (2000). Ethical climates and the ethical dimension of decision making. *Journal of Business Ethics*, 24, 125-140.

Kerfoot, K. (2004). The transparent organization: leadership in an open organization. *Medsurg Nursing*, 13(4), 267-268.

Motloung, M., & Lew, C. (2023). Drivers and consequences of strategic leader indecision: an exploratory study in a complex case. *Leadership & Organization Development Journal*.

Muna, F. A., & Mansour, N. (2009). Balancing work and personal life: The leader is an acrobat. *Journal of Management Development*, *28*(2), 121-133

Aldag, R., & Kuzuhara, L. (2015). *Creating high performance teams: Applied strategies and tools for managers and team members*. Routledge.

Alfrey, L. M. (2022). Diversity, Disrupted: A Critique of Neoliberal Difference in Tech Organizations. *Sociological Perspectives*, 65(6), 1081–1098. https://doi.org/10.1177/07311214221094664

Bottary, L. (2019, May 18). My favorite peer leadership story. *Vistage Research Center*. Retrieved August 18, 2023, from https://www.vistage.com/research-center/personal-development/favorite-peer-leadership-story/

Boskamp, E. (2023). 35+ Compelling Workplace Collaboration Statistics [2023]: The Importance Of Teamwork. Zippia. https://www.zippia.com/advice/workplace-collaboration-statistics/

Caulfield, B. (2011, May 9). Apple Blasts Past Google To Become World's Most Valuable Brand. *Forbes*. Retrieved August 17, 2023, from https://forbes.com/sites/briancaulfield/2011/05/09/apple-blasts-past-google-to-become-worlds-most-valuable-brand/amp/

Elkind, P. (2008). The trouble with Steve Jobs. *FORTUNE-EUROPEAN EDITION*, 157(5), 54.

Esberg, J. (2021, November 19). What the Facebook Whistleblower Reveals about Social Media and Conflict. *Crisis Group*. Retrieved August 17, 2023, from https://www.crisisgroup.org/united-states/united-states-internal/what-facebook-whistleblower-reveals-about-social-media-and-conflict

Gelbard, R. & Carmeli, A. (2009) The interactive effect of team dynamics and organizational support on ICT project success. *International Journal of Project Management*, 27, (5), 464-470. https://doi.org/10.1016/j.ijproman.2008.07.005

Momeny, L., & Gourgues, M. (2020). Communication that Develops Teams: Healthy Ministry Team Dynamics as a Function of Consistent Leader Communication of Emotional Intelligence. *Christian Education Journal*, 17(2), 283–297. https://doi.org/10.1177/0739891319876288

Nayak, P. R., & Ketteringham, J. (1997). 3M's Post-it notes: A managed or accidental innovation. *The human side of managing technological innovation*, 367-377.

Rather, A. Y. (2022). Salt as Symbol of Protest During the Dandi Satyagraha. *Journal of Legal Studies*, 2(3), 22-27.

Shah, R. (2020, December 24). Winning the "Just Do It" award by Jeff Bezos at Amazon. *Rajat Shah*. https://shahrajat.com/2020-12-24-amazon-just-do-it-award-jeff-bezos/

Eatough, E. (2022, October 11). 7 Ways to overcome fear of failure and move forward in life. *BetterUp*. Retrieved August 18, 2023, from https://www.betterup.com/blog/how-to-overcome-fear-of-failure

Fran. (2023, July 20). What is a growth mindset and how can you develop one? *FutureLearn*. Retrieved August 18, 2023, from https://www.futurelearn.com/info/blog/general/develop-growth-mindset

Ladd, H. (2023). How Much Of A Profit The Harry Potter Movies Made At The Box Office. *ScreenRant*. https://screenrant.com/harry-potter-movies-box-office-profit-explained/

References

Livingston, H. M., & Phillips, S. M. (2022). Courage: A key requirement for effective healthcare leadership. *Journal of Prosthodontic Research*, *66*(4), viii-x.

Morrison, A. S., & Heimberg, R. G. (2013). Social anxiety and social anxiety disorder. *Annual review of clinical psychology*, *9*, 249-274.

Ofili, P. (2018). Paradox of Barbarism and Fear in J. M. Coetzee's Waiting for the Barbarians. *Rhetor. Journal of the Canadian Society for the Study of Rhetoric*, *7*.

Robinson, L. (1990). Stress and anxiety. *Nursing Clinics of North America*, *25*(4), 935-943.

Willis, J. (2023). The GOAT: Why Michael Jordan is a Model for Business Owners and Entrepreneurs. *LinkedIn*. https://www.linkedin.com/pulse/goat-why-michael-jordan-model-business-owners-jon-willis

Angelica, A (2020, April 23)

3 Elevator pitch examples for students

https://slidebean.com/blog/elevator-pitch-examples-for-students

Blieck, De Anouk (2016, February 17)

Five ways to adapt to globalization and the changing workforce

https://www.frontiersin.org/articles/10.3389/fpsyg.2021.689671/full

Carucci, Ron(2022, April 10)

Why Leaders Need To Prioritize Their Team's Mental Health

https://www.forbes.com/sites/roncarucci/2022/04/10/why-leaders-need-to-prioritize-their-teams-mental-health/?sh=39a7d82f240d

Center for Creative Leadership

How to Build Your Leadership Image

https://www.ccl.org/articles/leading-effectively-articles/how-to-build-your-leadership-image/

Center for Management and Organizational Effectiveness

12 Reasons Ethical Leadership is Important in Business

https://cmoe.com/blog/12-reasons-ethical-leadership-is-important-in-business/

Cherry, K. (2023, February 24)

How Transformational Leadership Can Inspire Others

https://www.verywellmind.com/what-is-transformational-leadership-2795313

Deb, R (2023, January 20)

What is Sustainable Leadership and its Role in Shaping a Bright Future?

https://emeritus.org/blog/leadership-sustainable-leadership/

Denning, Steve (2021, May 14)

How New Leadership Succeeds In The Digital Age

https://www.forbes.com/sites/stevedenning/2021/03/14/how-new-leadership-succeeds-in-the-digital-age/?sh=110085f550a1

Haynie, Devon (2016, December 16)

Clocked out for Good

https://www.usnews.com/news/best-countries/articles/2016-09-16/worldwide-people-with-disabilities-struggle-to-find-jobs

Fonseca, W (2022, December 18)

Mastering the Elevator Pitch: Tips and Action Steps for Delivering a Confident and Effective Presentation

https://www.linkedin.com/pulse/mastering-elevator-pitch-tips-action-steps-delivering-fonseca-

Go-Business (2015, February 12)

Three Simple Steps to Adapt to Globalization

https://www.go-business.nl/index.php/2015/02/three-simple-steps-adapt-globalization/

Goldblatt, Craig (2020, April 17)

5 Simple Ways to Build Your Legacy

References

https://www.craiggoldblatt.com/5-simple-steps-to-build-your-legacy/

Grant, Triston (2023, January 1)

Combating Discrimination: Education and Empowerment for Social Change

https://www.voicesofyouth.org/blog/combating-discrimination-education-and-empowerment-social-change

Hewitt, L.N, (2018)

How do appearance and attitude impact leadership?

https://www.quora.com/How-do-appearance-and-attitude-impact-leadership

Hilary I. Lebow (2022, May 17)

Adapting to Change: Why It's Important and Tips to Do It

https://psychcentral.com/blog/adapting-to-change

Hinde and Sawyer (2023, June 5)

How can we empower the next generations to build a more sustainable future?

https://www.ey.com/en_gl/corporate-responsibility/empowering-next-generations-for-a-sustainable-future

Indeed (2022, June 25)

Crisis Leadership: Definition and 6 Essential Components

https://www.indeed.com/career-advice/career-development/crisis-leadership

Keates, C. (2019, April 29)

Four Steps To A Healthier Relationship With Technology

https://www.forbes.com/sites/forbescoachescouncil/2019/04/29/four-steps-to-a-healthier-relationship-with-technology/?sh=6ca069013e16

Kent State University

Your One-Minute Elevator Pitch

https://www.kent.edu/career/your-one-minute-elevator-pitch

KP&A (2022, May 3)

Balancing Life and Leadership

https://leadwithoutlimits.co.uk/2022/05/03/balancing-life-and-leadership/

Maldonado, A (2016, September 15)

Networking Skills: Elevator Pitch and the 5 Fundamental Pillars

https://www.linkedin.com/pulse/networking-skills-elevator-pitch-5-fundamental-annette-maldonado

Meyerhoefer, Franca L

Leadership in the Digital Age: How Technology is Changing the Game

https://www.speexx.com/speexx-blog/leadership-in-the-digital-age-how-technology-is-changing-the-game/

Newson, Andy J (2023, June 5)

Leading Through Change: 4 Strategies for Navigating Uncertainty

https://www.linkedin.com/pulse/leading-through-change-4-strategies-navigating-j-andy-newsom

Patel, Neil

Personal Branding: How to Go from Zero to Hero in No Time

https://neilpatel.com/blog/personal-branding/

ProResource (2020 April 1)

10 Ways Social Media Makes You a Better Leader

https://www.proresource.com/10-ways-social-media-makes-you-a-better-leader/

Robbins, Tony

How to Make a Positive Impact

https://www.tonyrobbins.com/leadership-impact/10-easy-ways-to-make-a-big-impact/

Rockwell, Dan (2014)

10 Ways to Build a Powerful Legacy Now

References

https://leadershipfreak.blog/2014/03/04/10-ways-to-build-powerful-legacy-now/?amp=1

Saadi, Melisa (2023, June 2)

The Transformative Power of Genuine Empathy in the Workplace

https://www.linkedin.com/pulse/transformative-power-genuine-empathy-workplace-saadi-guerbi-gphr-

Solanki, Baiju (2023, Jul 3)

The Ripple Effect of Empathy: 5 Ways in Which Compassionate Leadership Shapes a Positive Organizational Culture

https://www.linkedin.com/pulse/ripple-effect-empathy-5-ways-which-compassionate-baiju-solanki-

Sheninger, E (2016, January 8)

Your Digital Footprint Matters

https://www.huffpost.com/entry/your-digital-footprint-ma_b_8930874

Stone, Lira (2023, June 2)

Cultivating Empathy: The Hidden Superpower of Effective Leadership

https://medium.com/@meetlirastone/cultivating-empathy-the-hidden-superpower-of-effective-leadership-db15f256a631

Terzieva, K (2023, February 28)

The Rise Of Ethical Leadership In Modern Business Enterprises

https://www.forbes.com/sites/forbescoachescouncil/2023/02/28/the-rise-of-ethical-leadership-in-modern-business-enterprises/?sh=41bf75b237dd

Thompson, Debra (2021, May 11)

Balancing Leadership Responsibilities and Your Personal Life

https://www.linkedin.com/pulse/balancing-leadership-responsibilities-your-personal-life-thompson

University of Massachusetts Global

What is transformational leadership? Understanding the impact of inspirational guidance

https://www.umassglobal.edu/news-and-events/blog/what-is-transformational-leadership

Villirilli, G (2021, April 9)

The importance of being an ethical leader and how to become one

https://www.betterup.com/blog/the-importance-of-an-ethical-leader

Wade, Michael R. et al. (2017, March)

Redefining Leadership for a Digital Age

https://www.imd.org/research-knowledge/leadership/reports/redefining-leadership/

Weinstein, Bruce (2019, October 14)

Seven Bold Leaders Reveal How Ethical Leadership Is A Boon To Business

https://www.forbes.com/sites/bruceweinstein/2019/10/14/seven-bold-leaders-reveal-how-ethical-leadership-is-a-boon-to-business/?sh=29045caa454c

Xu, Binfeng et al. (2022, January 27)

How Environmental Leadership Boosts Employees' Green Innovation Behavior? A Moderated Mediation Model

https://www.frontiersin.org/articles/10.3389/fpsyg.2021.689671/full

(2022, December 6)

20 Teen Activists Who Inspire Us To Do More Good

https://www.goodgoodgood.co/articles/teen-activists

www.ingramcontent.com/pod-product-compliance
Lightning Source LLC
Chambersburg PA
CBHW060317050426
42449CB00011B/2527